# What Is Your Heritage and the State of Its Preservation?

*Volume 5*
*Connections to Place*

**Edited by**

**Barry L. Stiefel**

HERITAGE BOOKS
2022

**HERITAGE BOOKS**
***AN IMPRINT OF HERITAGE BOOKS, INC.***

**Books, CDs, and more—Worldwide**

For our listing of thousands of titles see our website
at
www.HeritageBooks.com

Published 2022 by
HERITAGE BOOKS, INC.
Publishing Division
5810 Ruatan Street
Berwyn Heights, Md. 20740



Heritage Books by the author:

*What Is Your Heritage and the State of Its Preservation?*

*Volume 1: Essays on Family History Exploration from the Field*

*Volume 2: Collaborations with Storyboard America*

*Volume 3: Putting Theory into Practice*

*Volume 4: Our Roots Run Deep*

*Volume 5: Connections to Place*

Front Cover Credit:
"Family Record", Terre-Haute, Indiana: J. M. Vickroy & Co., 1889.
Library of Congress, Prints and Photographs Division.



International Standard Book Number
Paperbound: 978-0-7884-2696-4

## Acknowledgments

Sincere thanks to Kimberly N. Morgan and Natalia Warchol of the *Finding Your Roots* documentary television series produce by McGee Media, for their generous support of this fifth volume of *What Is Your Heritage and the State of Its Preservation?: Connections to Place.* Your programming is a great inspiration to budding preservationists and genealogists.

# Table of Contents

## List of Figures

## Introduction

By Barry L. Stiefel

During the Spring 2022 semester several students at the College of Charleston's Historic Preservation and Community Planning program participated in their Senior Seminar titled "What Is *Your* Heritage and the State of Its Preservation?". This was the fifth time this seminar topic had been taught at the College of Charleston, with previous occurrences in 2014, 2016, 2018, and 2020. For this class, each student had to conduct an in-depth research paper on the state of preservation of heritage sites, material objects, or traditions associated with their family's history. The assignment used genealogical and family history research in an unconventional way by elevating the assessment of ancestors beyond typical names, dates, and generational succession; so commonly found on most family trees. The students had to ask profound questions to guide their inquiry, such as "Where (as in a specific spot) did my ancestors come from?"; "What was life like for them?"; and "What cultural traditions were important for them?". In this way the researcher became connected with their cultural forebearers, who are contextualized within time, place, and society. Moreover, the students had to utilize and synthesize the knowledge, skills, and experiences they acquired in previous classes. The class of 2022 was also able to read and discuss the essays of their predecessors from 2020, which were published in the fourth edited volume of this series.[1]

Following some understanding of their family history background the students then had to investigate "What is the current state of preservation?" of the places, customs, and artifacts related to their ancestor(s). They learned how to evaluate significance of place or artifact in respect to their family history, both within a personal framework as well as broader meaning within society as a whole. In some instances, the answer was easy because a student's ancestor of study was well known to contemporary historians, and the place(s), things, or customs associated with them were being well cared for. In other instances, students focused on a more vernacular past, where detailed records were often not readily available or never existed in the first place. While some students were descended from famous people of the past, it became important for the students to recognize the achievements of those whose names have almost or have become forgotten; especially considering that this is where the bulk of humanity comes from. Thus, the ethical question that was postulated, if one does not investigate and advocate for the preservation of one's own history and heritage, who will? And, if not now, when? Documenting our stories was the first step, and we all have a story to share.

Since this is the fifth volume of this series of published student papers, the subtitle of *Connections to Place* for the book has been used because of common underlying thread lines that connect the papers. The essays also have a geographical interest in the southern and eastern United States. Within this book are five essays volunteered by some of the students after the semester had ended, with each committing additional time for revision and research after graduation.

Madison Lee's *Through the Eyes of Appalachians: Why We Should Preserve Appalachian History* is the first chapter of this fifth volume. She has found that preserving Appalachian history is imperative in the context of American history. Previous research shows how coal companies and Big Pharma have taken advantage of the region, leaving Appalachia with more problems than solutions. In combination with the government and media's roles in the degradation of Appalachia, the region has suffered environmental degradation, high mortality rates, and poverty. Addressing these issues, can help people better understand Appalachia, rather than base their opinions on what is portrayed in television and "think pieces." Appalachia is not viewed as a preferred or ideal location for the majority of people to relocate to, and locals often flee the region, leaving those that stay with a lack of resources. Breaking down stereotypes and educating people about Appalachian culture can give people a deeper appreciation for the region, resulting in more people laying their roots in the region. Using genealogical databases, newspaper archives, and oral history, Lee gathered information about her family's history and their relationship to the region. She found a connection between her family's history, the coal industry, and the region's history with health and medicine, reflecting everyday struggles that most Appalachians of their generation faced. Finding significance in her own heritage helped Lee to have a deeper appreciation for where she came from and proved to her that preserving this type of heritage is necessary.

In *From Farming to Forestry,* by Chris Cone, the second chapter investigates the significance that land had for his ancestors, beginning from the time of their immigrant arrival in the early nineteenth century, followed by employment in agricultural, and then the eventual loss of land generations later. To do this, Cone investigated census records, newspaper articles, and family interviews that could give insight and context to life experiences of previous generations. He then evaluated his ancestors by separating them into different branches and explored each in more depth to find similarities and differences in their farming practices. This consisted of tenant farming, enslaving, and sharecropping, until the twentieth century, when some family members abandoned the land and others sold it. Within the interview process, Cone was able to uncover parallels in the stewardship of land that his family farmed and the preservation of memory from this agricultural past. Cone then concludes with his own thoughts on what remains for his family and the cultural landscapes that survive.

In the third chapter, Rebekah Seymour continues the scholarship on family connections to land in *Graniteville, South Carolina and the Importance of Small Town History*. This chapter discusses the shortage of knowledge on the history of small town America. While there are many small towns in the United States, Seymour feels this niche is underrepresented in American history. According to her, small towns have important cultural histories that are relevant to the nation as a whole, which is why Seymour uses her hometown of Graniteville, South Carolina as a case study. Graniteville is a mill town that her family has lived in for four generations since its founding in the nineteenth century. It was one of the first large-scale industrial production facilities in the South, which is additionally important because it was built at a time when the Southern elite directly opposed the importing of industrial practices. Graniteville is also important to the history of Southern education since it produced one of the first compulsory grade school system in the South. The town's founder, William Gregg, was influenced by utopian movements of the nineteenth century, which in turn had a lasting impact on the inhabitants of this town and their descendants for multiple generations.

In the next chapter, *The Klocks: Pioneers of the Mohawk Valley,* Gabriella Rowsam explores the surviving cultural landscapes of eighteenth century German Palatines communities, including her own ancestors, the Klocks. According to Rowsam's findings, German Palatines settlers were treated horribly by the British and years later set off on their own to settle in other areas of New York colony. The Klocks ended up permanently settling in the Mohawk River Valley, where they lived on frontier land. Through literature, historic documents, and a fortified homestead, this chapter delves into the forgotten lineage of the Klock family; how they came to settle in the Mohawk River Valley in New York, their involvement in the French & Indian War and the American Revolution, and what material remains survive as a means to educate present generations about the past.

The last chapter *A Hellene in Hell's Kitchen: Greek Perspectives of Ethnicity and Homeland in Twentieth Century America,* by Noah Sigalas, follows the experience of Greek immigrants in the United States. Sigalas asks, what does it mean for our past to act in our lives, and how does this shape our identities? Identity is a hot topic today, but the way it interacts and evolves over time is infrequently discussed. For Sigalas, this boiled down to his Greek ethnic background. "What does it mean for him to be of Greek extraction while living in America?" is a question that he explores. Though his specific background may not be shared by all, going through this journey of self-discovery can assist others in helping to discover something about themselves.

In closing, this sample of papers reflects the students who volunteered their research from the Spring 2022 semester. A list of the other papers is included to demonstrate the breadth and diversity of the students who took the class and decided not to publish. It is our hope – both my own as well as the students' – that our work can serve as an inspiration to others to think more comprehensively about one's own family history and cultural heritage. To think beyond names, dates, and generational succession so that the lives of our ancestors can be better understood; to begin processes of reconciliation because of new perspectives about the past not previously considered; as well as to foster and promote the preservation of the places, heirlooms, and traditions we have inherited today for future generations.

## List of Student Papers Not Published From 2022:

| | |
|---|---|
| Keelie Britt | *Stories Are the New Heirlooms* |
| Jenna Chalhoub | *From Syria to America in the Early Twentieth Century* |
| Cole Hair | *Southern Ties* |
| Skyler Lee | *Harvested Memories: The Decay of Rural Duford and the Pasts of Those Grown Here* |
| Savannah Lied | *The Reich Family's Blend of German and Pennsylvania Dutch Heritage: A Story About Small-Town Roots* |
| Helen McGaughy | *Ancestral Structures and the Stories they Tell* |
| Femi Olalere | *The Olalere's Journey from Ibadan, to Lagos, to Charleston* |
| Julia Rozin | *L'dor V'dor: Food & Thoughts from Generation to Generation* |
| Jessica Stech | *My Family History and Cultural Traditions* |
| Jack Sutton | *Fripp Island: Sand Dunes and Suttons* |
| Darby Toole | *The Seeds My Father Sewed for Me* |
| Cate Venturini | *My Italian Heritage and its Preservation: The Ties Between Food, Family, and Traditions* |
| Lindsey Weinstein | *Heritage's Through My Artistic Expression* |

Figure 0.1: The Caroline and Albert Simons Jr. Center for Historic Preservation at the College of Charleston, where the students spent a significant amount of time on their Bachelor of Arts degrees in Historic Preservation and Community Planning. Photograph by the editor.

# Chapter 1: Through the Eyes of Appalachians: Why We Should Preserve Appalachian History

By Madison Lee

There is a place where the people are embraced by the mountains. They are enwrapped in the chirping of birds, the tickle of grass between their toes, and the aroma of honeysuckles. Nature is embedded in the culture, at-home remedies are considered medicine, and the people display strength and hardiness. This place is Appalachia. It is a region of mountains that spans across thirteen states in parts of the northeastern and eastern United States. Both of my parents are from the region. My mother was raised on a dairy farm in Dayton, Virginia, and my father grew up in a little place called Briary Branch, located in Rockingham County, Virginia. Appalachia has always been a huge part of my family's life. It is where my parents come from, so we have naturally returned many times, and there was a brief five years in my childhood that we lived there. Listening to Bluegrass music, sipping moonshine, cultivating gardens, and fishing have always been a part of how my family bonds. As someone who considers Appalachian culture a part of my heritage, I am familiar with the ways the federal government has failed the region over time. Because of the region's past, preserving Appalachian history is often not appreciated or recognized. Using my ancestor's stories: Catherine Bradford, her husband, James Lawrence Lee (who was injured in the mines and left paralyzed), and his father, John Dove Lee (a coal company doctor). From these case studies, I will share the struggles of this region and culture, and explain why preserving this history is important.

**Background**

Appalachia spans north from New York state and south, down to Alabama, following the mountain chain by this name. The Appalachian region has less to do with its defined geographical location, more to do with the culture of its inhabitants. Due to the region's isolation provided by the mountains and natural topography, Appalachia developed its own distinct culture and traditions. The Shenandoah Valley is the portion of Appalachia I am most familiar with, and where my parents, grandparents, and great grandparents have all called home. The Shenandoah Valley is located between the Blue Ridge Mountains and the Allegheny mountains, and stretches from Augusta County, Virginia to Jefferson County, West Virginia.[1] Augusta County is where I lived for part of my childhood and will always hold a special place in my heart. Rockingham County is adjacent to Augusta County and is home to Harrisonburg and the high school that my parents attended. Boone County is in West Virginia, where my great-grandmother served as mayor for the small town of Sylvester, with a population of 171 people in 2020.[2] Most of the Shenandoah Valley consists of small towns sporadically scattered across the rural landscape.

During the summers, towns in the valley throw "lawn parties" in which the whole town gets together to celebrate the warm weather. Lawn parties typically last a week and share a similar concept of a county fair. To kick off the week of summertime events, there is a procession that comes through the town's main street. The procession includes local boy and girl scouts, dance teams, floats featuring inflatable animals, and the occasional horse and buggy. After the procession, everyone gathers at the "lawn," which is usually a grassy lot nearby. The lawn is covered with carnival games and rides, vendors selling their homemade apple butter and pork rinds, and tractors. People often use their tractors as their main mode of transportation to the event, as well as to show them off or even sell them. Animals are also a featured part of the festivities; people often bring their prize pig or cow to compete in Future Farmers of America's livestock show. The lawn parties are when the community gets together to enjoy the warm weather, but also enjoy all that Shenandoah has to offer.

While my anecdote may give a picturesque view of small town living, there is more to know about Appalachia and the Shenandoah Valley. In the eighteenth century there were several waves of Ulster-Scots (Scots-Irish) migrating to America due to religious tension, economic instability, and crop failure in Ulster. When they got to America, the Scots-Irish settled in what we now called Appalachia because of land availability. Much of what we consider "folk" or Appalachian culture derived from the Scots-Irish, such as the preference of ballads and songs like "Barbara Allen" or "Tom Dooley." Fiddling, clogging, specific dialects, and even the ideology of clans influenced by Scots-Irish settlers.[3]

The Swiss and Germans also have roots in the Shenandoah Valley's heritage and had a great impact on the architectural types of the valley. The stone-and-log *Flurkuchenhaus,* which features three rooms, centered around a chimney and sometimes a corner staircase, was a popular architectural type during the area's settlement.[4] The Lewis Shuey House in Augusta County is a great example of this style of architecture, constructed circa 1795 for Revolutionary War veteran, Lewis Shuey, whose grandfather migrated from the Rhineland Palatinate region to Pennsylvania, only to later relocate again to Augusta County.[5] However, the English I-house grew more popular in the decades to follow. The Pennsylvania barn also became a common type of structure in the region; derived from Swiss architecture that uses the lands topography to create access to a second level, as the barns are banked into a hillside.[6] The cultural exchange between the Swiss, Scots-Irish, and German settlers, in addition to their shared agricultural experiences, contributed to the greater Shenandoah Valley-Appalachian cultural heritage.

Appalachia is not a region with an all-white population, with contributions from people of color. Native Americans have lived in Appalachia long before European settlers began venturing into the region.[7] As the settlers came to the region, so did free and enslaved Blacks. Before a "racial hierarchy" had been established in the region, Native Americans, Blacks, and European settlers lived in communities together. White and Black Appalachians bonded over playing music, thus the introduction of the banjo, an instrument that roots lead back to Africa. While Andrew Jackson's Indian Removal Act of 1830 pushed the majority of Native Americans west, African Americans remained a part of Appalachian society. During the Great Migration, there was an influx of Blacks to work in the coal mines, as it was rumored that the coal miners in Appalachia received better working conditions and higher wages than in the South. African Americans and Native Americans were actively sought after for coal mining jobs to work alongside white coal miners, to create language barriers within the workplace in hopes that it would prevent unionization. In the 1950s, strip mining replaced deep mining, so the coal companies laid off many Black coal miners because they did not feel that they could hire them as machine operators. The layoffs resulted in some African Americans leaving the region to find jobs in northern cities. Today, Appalachia is experiencing an influx of immigrants from Eastern Europe and Latin America.[8]

**Poverty**

Appalachia has widely been disenfranchised in the United States, primarily the central region, which is made up by 82 counties from Kentucky, West Virginia, Virginia, and Tennessee. Cara Robinson explains that people of Central Appalachia "lower educational rates, lower income and wealth, higher levels of obesity and disease and less access to long term, stable middle class wages and jobs than the majority of American communities." [9] Central Appalachia is known as an internal colony, meaning that its people have been exploited by a majority within the United States.[10] The United States government and large corporations, many that have been backed by politicians, have exploited the economic, social, and natural resources of the sub-region for decades.[11] Specifically the coal industry exploited the region's resources, land, and people. Unfortunately, the people of Appalachia have also experienced perpetual poverty. In addition to the region's checkered history with the coal industry, the area also suffers from digital inequality. With the introduction of the internet, there were concerns of equitable access to the internet.[12]

Now that finding internet access is less of an issue, the question of "what they are able to do when they go online?" has now been asked. It has been discovered that there is a large gap in how middle and upper class citizens use the internet versus those of impoverished backgrounds. [13] Middle and upper class people are more likely to use the internet for economic and educational purposes, such as searching for employment opportunities, networking, online courses and civic engagement. [14] Because it took longer to introduce the internet to central Appalachia, and that many of the people in the community are impoverished and cannot afford the latest technological advancements, they are often behind on the learning curve with new technology and information.[15] Today, organizations like the Central Appalachian Regional Network and the Appalshop have been working to fight for digital equality in the region.

In addition to digital and technological inequities, the region also suffers from a plethora of other factors contributing to its poverty rates. Since 1980 the United States job opportunities have skyrocketed to 79 percent, while in Appalachia jobs have only increased by 49 percent. [16] Appalachians have been disproportionately affected by the loss of job opportunities in the coal mining and manufacturing industries. Post-secondary education fulfillment is another category in which Appalachians fall short, and it is not because people in the region are unable to receive acceptance into four year colleges. From 2015 to 2019, the number of Appalachians that had received a bachelor's degree or more, was 7 percent points lower than the national average.[17] In that same time period, less than one-fifth of people in the region 25 years and older had at least four years of college education. Many Appalachians cannot afford higher education because of the need to provide for their families, which creates a vicious cycle.

The region also lacks in basic infrastructure, "roughly 20% of the region's population is not served by a community water system (compared with 12% nationally), and 47% of Appalachian households are not served by a public sewage system (compared with 24% nationally)." When I had lived in the Shenandoah Valley, my family did not have water provided by a community water system, rather we had a well that was costly to maintain. The well water would often smell of rotten eggs or sulfur. I never realized how much I had taken for granted the water systems provided by municipal utilities. Another factor that contributes to Appalachia's economic success is access to reliable and safe transportation. The completion of the Appalachian Development Highway System and the creation of more railways, marine/inland ports, roads, and airports are examples of ways to make rural communities more interconnected with each other as well as contribute to (re)vitalizing the local economies.[18] Many Appalachian communities do not have the bandwidth for planning, developing, and funding to drive economic (re)development at the local level. Implementing the capacity for building, planning, and technical assistance could foster more viable economic development for the region.[19]

Appalachia remains one of the most impoverished regions in the United States and continues to face the negative impacts from the coal industry and internal colonialism. Although the internet has provided a gateway for Appalachians to break away from isolation and engage with mainstream American society, it has also perpetuated poverty through digital inequality.[20] To get the region out of economic distress, the federal government needs to help end the cycle of poverty. By no means does poverty define Appalachian identity, it is just a hurdle that the region hopes to overcome. With the help of policymakers acknowledging the inequalities in the region, reparations can be made to lessen the gap between Appalachians and the majority of Americans.

**Health & Medicine**

For the majority of Appalachian's history post-European settlement, modern medicine has not been readily available in most of the rural areas. The healthcare that is provided in the small towns is either sparse, poor quality or lacking resources. People like my maternal grandfather have died because an ambulance could not get there in time because the nearest public hospital was too far away. In a report conducted by the Walsh Center for Rural Health Analysis at NORC at the University of Chicago, data collected between 2014 and 2015 shows that "overall mortality in Appalachia is increasing at a faster rate than in the non-Appalachian United States, which suggests the increasing mortality rate in the Appalachian Region is contributing to the increase in overall mortality in the United States."[21] This can be attributed to higher rates of drug overdose, suicide, and alcoholic liver disease, as seen in a chart from this report. It does not stop there. I also came across reports about the region's struggles with obesity, diabetes, heart disease, cancer, and HPV. These health and mortality concerns could be mended "by improving educational opportunities and achievement; reducing poverty; and providing stable housing, transportation, and labor market opportunities."[22]

Despite the modern problems Appalachian's face when it comes to health care access, they have historically always had this issue as the mountains cause isolation and seclusion that made access to medical care difficult. Over time, people developed remedies and other forms of self-prescribed medicine. Many Appalachians have relied on midwives or local healers for medical needs, and these people that acted as individual practitioners were highly respected in the community. Remedies are usually passed down by oral transmission from generation to generation. The ingredients for most remedies are household items such as vinegar, baking soda, salt, sugar, herbs, toothpaste, and nail polish– items that are easily accessible.[23] I once read an oral history in which a local medicine woman from Shull's Mill, North Carolina, named Mamie Graybeal Shull, used motor oil to treat a poison ivy rash:

> Now, it will stain your bed, it will just stain everything. Dean used to have it so bad, and Pappy said to me one time 'If you would take some old motor oil and grease him. Take some old rags and wrap around it because it will stain your bedclothes, and that will cure him.[24]

Folk medicine can mean anything from rubbing Vick's vapor rub on a facial blemish to making sassafras tea for a little energy boost. Appalachian folk medicine is an example of how mountain folk adapted to the isolation using the resources they had. It also speaks to how the culture of the region is rooted in kinship ties. By passing remedies from generation to generation or sharing remedies with neighbors it creates a bond that weaves those kinship ties even tighter.

Sassafras roots and mushroom tea can't fix everything, leaving some people to turn to other forms of self-medicating. Due to the region's poverty, many go uninsured and those that are insured often struggle due to the lack of access to healthcare in rural areas. In *Rural Mental Health,* they attribute the substance abuse problem in Appalachia to:

1. Lack of access to health professionals because of cost and insufficient health insurance coverage
2. Lack of access to qualified health care providers as a result of travel distance, lack of training in evidence-based and evidence-supported treatments, and/or lack of trust in health professionals to provide effective treatment.
3. Lack of educational and economic opportunity contributing to systemic poverty, a key determinant of high substance abuse.[25]

The opioid epidemic has gotten out of control in the United States, and Appalachian communities are struggling to cope with the increasing rates of addiction and overdoses. As someone that has a brother that struggles with drug-use and alcohol abuse, I have a deep understanding of what addiction looks like and how painful it can be for a person suffering with addiction and their loved ones. In Appalachia, far too many people share my experience, and the only way to combat this problem is by getting to the source.

Big pharmaceutical companies such as Purdue Pharma have taken advantage of the lack of access to health care in Appalachia and pushed addictive opioids like OxyContin on rural Americans for far too long.[26] What happens when these potentially fatal narcotics enter Appalachian communities? People are often prescribed larger doses and quantities than needed, and trusting patients take home these opioids with little advising. In a study conducted by the Appalachian Regional Commission (ARC) and Oak Ridge Associated Universities (ORAU) many Appalachians have reported being over prescribed opioids, and even been called "crazy" for questioning the doctor about the prescription. [27] In this study only two out of 47 participants were even counseled when prescribed opioids; so many times patients are being prescribed opioids and not being advised of the side effects, whether they are safe to mix with alcohol or other substances, nor do they understand how truly addictive they can be. There is also the challenge of "pill mills," places where community members know they can get prescriptions for whatever they want from an unethical physician. To make matters worse, few doctors were held accountable by the law for these horrific drug crimes.[28]

Appalachian health care professionals have taken note of the impacts of the opioid crisis. It has resulted in an increase in overdoses and fatalities, as well as higher rates of Hepatitis C, HIV, neonatal abstinence syndrome, dental problems, mental health issues and suicide, malnourishment, and automobile accidents. Unfortunately, the region lacks proper access to programs that could remedy this crisis such as "non-narcotic alternatives to addressing pain management such as physical therapy, acupuncture, and cognitive-behavioral therapy and local, affordable, and licensed programs for treatment of opioid addiction."[29] In order to combat this crisis the ARC and the ORAU have made recommendations for preventive measures such as community outreach programs, youth based initiatives, and working with both healthcare providers and law enforcement to provide more educational and training opportunities. Community support systems can be helpful for remedying this crisis, but they need to be used in conjunction with proper education, policy, and healthcare assistance.

**Exploitation of the Area**

Coal has been at the heart of many Appalachian communities, especially those in the central region. Coal mining has been responsible for the region's economic development, as well as its destruction and destitution. The industry not only changed the lives of male laborers in Appalachia, but women and children too. Coal companies used Appalachians for cheap labor, destroyed their land, polluted the region, and opposition to the coal companies often led to violence. After the Civil War, a new era of agricultural and industrial advancements began to take off. Railroads began to reach into Appalachia, which led to the introduction of coal towns and logging camps.[30] The companies that set up in Appalachia were usually not from the region, so profits were sent out of the region's economy while little money was being dispersed into Appalachia's economy. Both coal and lumber companies extracted land from inhabitants. Local entrepreneurs often gave the companies leads on who had land, and what it would take for them to sell their land. However, as the tensions arose between property owners and outside companies, people became more hesitant to give up their land. According to Chad Montrie, coal mining company agents pressured local residents that refused to sell:

> Ownership of property in the region was often uncertain because of confusion surrounding the

> original grants and the subsequent purchase of the land by other settlers or occupation by squatters. Land titles were obscure, deeds were lost, and records were poor in most mountain counties. Speculators with a better understanding of laws, courts, and the workings of local and state governments used their knowledge and connections to their own advantage. As a result, by 1910 outlanders controlled not only the best stands of hardwood timber and the thickest seams of coal but a large percentage of the surface land in the region as well.[31]

Deep mining and surface mining were being used to obtain coal in Appalachia, but surface coal mining gained much more traction in the twentieth century. In the mid-1970s there was the introduction of the process of "mountaintop removal" to obtain coal, which is a form of surface mining that destroys mountaintops and ridgelines.[32] Mountaintop removal is blasting the peaks of mountains off, which can be as harmful to its surrounding areas as it sounds. Mountaintop removal can loosen the foundations of homes and buildings nearby, create health risks (asthma, cancer, respiratory problems), pollute the environment, cause mudslides, and kill or displace wildlife.[33] Mountaintop removal is responsible for ruining Appalachia's picturesque natural landscape, and many Appalachians, who value the environment, were appalled by the destruction created by the coal mining industry.

One of Massey Energy's subsidiaries had a coal preparation plant in Raleigh County, West Virginia only a few hundred feet from Marsh Fork Elementary School. While the plant is no longer in operation 2.8 billion gallons of coal sludge sits at the top of the hill.[34] My paternal grandfather, John Lee was a student at Marsh Fork Elementary and his mother grew up in Marsh Fork, so this story sits deep with me.[35] Students were finding coal dust on surfaces throughout the school and parents were afraid to send their children to school when it rained, because they feared the impoundment would break. When an impoundment breaks the sludge could roll down the hill destroying the school, killing everyone in its path, and leaving the water contaminated. It wasn't until 2013 that they built a new school a few miles away.[36] Young children were put at risk for decades, before anything was done about the issue.

Beyond the health risks, visual blight, and the environmental impacts, coal companies took advantage of the people in central Appalachian communities. Coal companies would build company towns, which were clusters of small, cheaply-built houses that would be in close proximity to each other and close to the coal mines so there was no need for automobiles and workers would not have a reason to be late for their duties.[37] Company towns operated on company currency which could only be used at company stores. This system perpetuated poverty and made the workers and their families dependent on the coal companies. People would risk being fired or sent to prison if they were found buying or selling outside of company stores. Poverty led to starvation and starvation, led to loss of morality. People began to steal which only contributed to the stereotype of "hillbilly thieves."[38]

There was some opposition to the coal companies because coal workers were working under dangerous conditions with low wages and no benefits. Coal workers were being exploited, and this led to the coal wars, which entailed protests, strikes, and unionization. What many people fail to realize is that women were at the center of these movements; they saw the abuse and ill treatment of their brothers, fathers, husbands, and sons and were motivated to fight back. During the strikes of 1973 in Harlan County, the women of Brookside even fought against "the gender and class fault lines in the capitalist coal industry," as their unpaid reproductive labor was fueling the coal industry's labor force. The women knew their role was vital to the coal companies, but they were growing tired of the companies creating a suffocating and toxic environment for them and their families.[39] It is important to recognize that women were not just voicing their opinions and organizing behind the scenes, they were actively on the picket lines. It was illegal for more than three miners to strike at a time, so as a loophole the women participated instead.

Many strikes would get violent, but when women were on the scene, strikebreakers were less likely to use gun violence. Many believe if the women had not participated the strikes would have been bloodier, and the participation of women also showed the rest of the nation how intense things had gotten in Appalachia. The strikers would not back down, and in 1974 the United Mine Workers of America finally had their agreement signed by the Eastover Mining Company. Protesters like Bessie L. Cornett faced violence and backlash from family and neighbors for participating in the strikes.[40] Cornett recalled her husband telling her,

> 'You can't go' [participate in the strike]. He even beat me or locked the doors. He said a woman's role was in the home, cooking and cleaning and so on. And there was a lot of jealousy. If you were exposed to a lot of other social activities, you might begin to broaden your interests a little outside of the home and see that you had more potential.[41]

Appalachian women were gaining their voice, standing up for their beliefs, and fighting structural oppression, and the violence and alienation that came with it.

## My Appalachian Roots

Growing up I was told my great-grandmother, Cate, was a lot of things: a former mayor of her small town, a person with grit and tenacity, and a doting grandmother; but she had her faults and secrets. I always knew that out of everyone in my father's family, he was the closest to her and he never let the negatives impact his angelic view of her. I remember visiting her as a child and seeing my father light up around her. The only time I ever saw my father cry was when he heard of her passing. Grandma Cate was the matriarch of the family in my father's eyes. Catherine Evelyn Bradford was born February 6, 1927, in Huntington, West Virginia.[42] Her father was a barber, and her mother was a stay at home mother. Cate also had three siblings.[43]

According to my father, Cate worked as a nurse and at one point was running a florist shop out of her house. He told me how he remembered visiting and seeing refrigerators storing flowers everywhere.[44] She exuded independence and had a drive to provide for her family the best she could, even if it meant running a business out of her home. In 1947, she married my great-grandfather, James Lawrence Lee, the adopted son of a coal mining physician, Dr. John Dove Lee.[45] James met my great- grandmother at a local dance hall after he was discharged from the Navy in 1946.[46] In the Navy, James worked as a hospital apprentice, which I personally feel was inspired by his father's work in the medical field.[47] He was injured in World War II and came back to work in the coal mines. Unfortunately, he was involved in a coal mining accident that left him paralyzed from the waist down.[48] Coal mining wives, like my great-grandmother, understood that when their husbands went off to work, they were facing dangerous conditions and there was always a possibility that they would not be home for supper.

In Carol A.B. Giesen's *Coal Miner's Wives: Portraits of Endurance,* a woman she interviewed discussed the hardships of being a coal miner's wife:

> You have to get used to having your husband come home so tired he can't do anything. You got to get used to him being so dirty it doesn't come out of his skin. Or having him come home sometimes with a wrenched back or smashed fingers or telling you that someone you know got hurt today and he's lucky it wasn't him.[49]

The life of a coal miner's wife comes with anxiety, coping, and learning to cope. It did not matter if a coal miner's wife worked a full-time or part-time job, at the end of the day she still would consider herself a full-time homemaker. [50] I imagine that my great-grandfather's accident put strain on my great-grandmother and the family. She had to provide money for the household, while simultaneously running the house; doing the brunt of the chores, caring for the children, and cooking meals. During this time, anti-poverty and welfare rights activists were pushing for caregiving to be a larger part of the American dialogue as it is associated with solving poverty, environmental issues, labor struggles, women's rights, and even democratic participation in communities.

Unfortunately, most working mothers faced hardships in American workplaces, as they did not accommodate their roles as caregivers– this created a shift in Americans' relationship to work. [51] After recovering from the accident, my great grandparents moved their family to Illinois where James went back to school to get his law degree.[52] He then got a job as an attorney for the Commonwealth of Virginia, so they moved to Richmond. [53] Around this time, my great-grandmother illegally used the alias "Evelyn Catherine Bradford" to marry another man, James Hugh Stone; the marriage was annulled as she was still legally married to James at the time.[54] My father says that she only married Stone because he was a paraplegic as well, and she wanted to collect benefits from both marriages.[55] In Appalachia, poverty makes people desperate at times; While I am not sure if she married for love or money, I could understand how a woman nursing her newly paraplegic husband, supporting the family financially, and caring for children may have been overwhelming and driven her to commit fraud.

I was not surprised to learn this information about my grandmother, as a few months ago after my grandfather's passing, his sisters took DNA tests and learned they had different fathers. There were always rumors that she had fathered all of her children with different men, and she was known for having affairs. While I do not condone being unfaithful to someone, I have never put any fault or blame on her. I imagine being a woman during that time was difficult. If she was unhappy in her marriage, I imagine she had her reasons and constraints that prevented her from leaving, whether it was religion, financial stability, her children, or even society. I always admired how this part of her history never impacted the way my father viewed her.

James Lawrence died in 1968 at the age of 42. My father said his passing was related to complications he had faced as a paraplegic. My great-grandmother remarried twice after my great-grandfather's death. My father remembers visiting her and her second (legal) husband, Bob Milam, who always was sure to give my father a silver dollar when he saw him.[56] After he passed, she remarried Bob McClain, who also passed leaving my great-grandmother a three-time widow. Some may find it difficult to fathom how a woman could have three of her husbands' pass away, but in West Virginia the life expectancy is much lower than the rest of the United States. In a study analyzed by the National Center for

Health Statistics, West Virginia ranked 50$^{th}$ out of all of the states with and the District of Columbia, with an average life expectancy of 74.5 years as of 2019; for men specifically, the life expectancy is 71.9 years in West Virginia.[57] I am uncertain as to what Milam and McClain did for a living, there is a strong possibility that they were subjected to the impacts of the coal industry or the general lack of healthcare in Appalachia.

Healthcare was an important aspect of my family's history. As previously mentioned, Cate was a nurse when she was young, James worked as a hospital apprentice in the Navy, and James' father John Dove Lee was a doctor for Raleigh-Wyoming Coal Company.[58] My great-great grandfather, John Dove Lee attended the College of Charleston and then graduated from the Southern College of Medicine and Surgery, located in Atlanta, in 1912.[59] He was about 24 years old when he graduated medical school, which may appear to be baffling today, but in 1880 a doctor would attend a preparatory school for two years, followed by two years of medical school.[60] My paternal grandfather, or as I called him, Papa John always told us the story about how he was born in his grandfather's house. My father would then remind us that Papa John's grandfather was a doctor and he operated out of his home regularly, so it was not as shocking as he made it sound to us children. The majority of coal towns in West Virginia were small communities and could not house a regular medical practice, so coal doctors were the primary doctors for more than just the coal miners, but the whole community.

Coal company doctors are not how you would envision doctors today, in white lab coats working in sterile environments with all the gleaming silver, disinfected tools and monitors, working alongside a team of nurses. Coal doctors, like Dr. John Dove, would work out of their homes. Their kitchen table would serve as an operating table, their den as a waiting room, their wives or friends acting as nurses and assistants.[61] My father remembered his father telling him stories about how he would assist his grandfather with patients, and how the most gruesome coal mining injuries would haunt him. Unlike other coal doctors, Dr. John Dove employed a nurse and performed surgeries; he even flew a flag with a red cross on it during the Great Depression, to let people know passing by that he could offer medical care. He was known for helping the community and feeding anyone with an empty belly, even if all he had to offer was baked beans.[62]

By the mid 1930s, miners were growing dissatisfied with the healthcare system put in place by the coal companies; they viewed it as paternalistic and unfair.[63] The companies created a system where miners would get a deduction from their paychecks to cover their medical expenses for the month, called a checkoff. Some companies would give the doctor the entire check off, while other coal companies would keep 10 to 20 percent of the profit and give the rest to the doctor.[64] Most miners were not pleased that they did not have a choice as to who their healthcare provider was, nor did they receive any hospital services through the coal company. There was an obvious fear that the coal company doctors only served those who hired and paid them, rather than the patients they saw. Many times doctors were encouraged to prevent people from passing screenings, because the coal companies did not want to risk employing any laborers that may be a liability or require any medical attention. This system prevented many able-bodied men from being able to work and provide for their families, as well as discriminated against those with disabilities.[65]

The healthcare system devised by the coal companies was only one of numerous ways that the industry took advantage of the people. They found ways to make the people in coal towns completely reliant on their systems, which only perpetuated poverty in these small, isolated communities. Eventually, miners pushed for union control over checkoffs and the ability to choose their provider, some unions even established their own hospitals to provide proper healthcare for the miners.[66] In addition to the role that healthcare plays in my family's narrative, both my great-grandmother Cate and her father-in-law John Dove were actively involved in community affairs and local politics. Cate was the mayor of her small town in West Virginia, Sylvester.[67] I was unable to find any factual information that would corroborate that she was actually elected, but the records in small town Appalachia are pretty lacking or not digitized yet.

Cate was known for slinging around her title as former mayor of Sylvester. In a story that my father once told me, she was riding as a passenger in my Papa John's car and my father was in the backseat when they were pulled over by the police for speeding. When the police officer approached the car she told him, "Do you know who I am? I am the former mayor of Sylvester and I used to own you cops. You oughta' be ashamed of yourselves for setting up a speed trap like that!"[68] She was a firecracker, and her confrontation with the police resulted in Papa John receiving a ticket in which he had to appear in court for. Despite trying to use her political background to persuade police out of giving a speeding ticket, she was a pillar in her community and on the board of the PTA for the local school district.[69]

John Dove was known for serving his community, offering medical services or a warm meal to anyone that needed it.[70] He also ran as a democratic candidate for the House of Delegates in 1956.[71] From the stories I have been told, John Dove was someone that people in the community really relied on and trusted. Both Cate and John Dove were Baptist Democrats, which shocked me to my core because growing up I knew my grandfather,

Papa John, as a Mormon Republican.[72] Appalachians are often painted as white, conservative, often uneducated people, and for the most part I saw my father's family to fit the stereotype. My father had never told me about how his grandparents and great grandparents often quarreled with his father about his political views until I began collecting oral histories.

Many people, including myself, do not realize that West Virginia's coal country was primarily Democratic for forty years. [73] Both Democratic and Republican politicians in West Virginia have blamed the "war on coal" on overregulation, and ignoring that the industry decline was actually due to competition and economic factors. Both parties also agreed that "the way forward requires the free flow of capital in the hands of businesses, not people." [74] There was little difference between party candidates, and West Virginians displayed pretty apathetic behavior when it came to politics.[75] The 2016 presidential election changed West Virginian voters and the way the rest of the nation viewed Appalachia.

**Modern Appalachia**

Today, we think of Appalachia as "Trump Country," the land of angry conservatives wearing bright red hats. To understand Appalachia better, you have to recognize what led the region to light up red and how the 2016 Presidential election impacted Appalachia. Appalachian voices are often glazed over, their stories go untold, and problems go unsolved– even in articles and think pieces about Appalachian during the election, their voices are absent.[76] West Virginians faced alienation and indifference from former political candidates, so when Donald Trump told the people he was a candidate for the working class it made Appalachians feel as though they would finally gain their voice in the political arena.[77] The media ran with the narrative that Appalachians represented the dark parts of America, and labeling the region as "Trump Country" only alienated the region more.[78] Many Appalachians supported Trump in the 2016 election, and they justified their support with "alienation from both parties, triggered by unmet political expectations and white racial anxiety."[79]

Racial anxiety is when heightened stress is associated with interacting with someone outside one's race. People of color experience this in fear of facing discrimination or malice based on their race, while white people fear being perceived as racist.[80] However, the reasons they used to justify their support were exclusive to Appalachian voters, supporters of Trump outside the region shared much of the same justifications. Hillary Clinton's comments at a CNN sponsored town-hall meeting only rationalized the Appalachian voter's choice more, "I'm the only candidate which has a policy about how to bring economic growth using clean renewable energy as the key into coal country… Because we're going to put a lot of coal miners and coal companies out of business, right?"[81] She continued, but the nail was already in the coffin, "And we're going to make it clear that we don't want to forget those people. Those people labored in those mines for generations, losing their health, often losing their lives to turn on our lights and power our factories."[82] This was a real turning point in the campaign. Clinton had only maintained the idea that Appalachians were excluded from the mainstream by referring to them as "those people" multiple times, not to mention she lost a lot of respect and trust from coal mining families. The media has always painted Appalachians as "ignorant, racist, appalled by the idea of a female President or a black President, suspicious and frightened of immigrants and Muslims, with a threatened job or no job at all, addicted to OxyContin," to separate them from the rest of American society. Labeling the area as "Trump Country" is another way the media has perpetuated the "otherness" surrounding Appalachians.[83]

## Moving Forward

Throughout my examination of Appalachia, I have explained the atrocities the region has faced, the strength and tenacity of the people, and my own personal experiences; the intention is not to induce pity or shame, but rather to understand the region and gain appreciation for its resilience despite everything it has faced. Appalachians take pride in their home. Nature is ingrained in who they are. They take pride in community and helping one another. The region's isolation has created some blinders in that some Appalachians may be considered below the poverty line on a national scale, but they do not view themselves as poor. Many Appalachians do not realize they are poor until they leave the region, or in today's world, see it on social media. Growing up in Appalachia, children are happy frolicking bare foot in cow pastures and wading in rivers alongside catfish three times their size. It is not until they mature, they are told to get out of the region and find something better and bigger for themselves. An internal weight of shame grows; the places they have called home and loved are suddenly supposed to be a place to despise and leave. For young LGBTQ+ members, the self-marginalization is even greater. They hold an appreciation for their home, but there is the issue that their home might not love them back. They flee the region to find places where they think they will belong, often urban areas, where the culture is extremely different and can be difficult to adjust to. Luckily there are ongoing efforts to disrupt the pattern of internalized shame, as well as encourage the public embrace of Appalachia cultural heritage.

## Preserving Appalachian Heritage

Davis & Elkins College in Elkins, West Virginia has done an exemplary job of executing preservation of pieces of Appalachian heritage and culture. The college hired a preservation consultant to ensure that items are being properly assessed and preserved. [84] Davis and Elkins has collected a volume of film, recordings, oral histories, photographs, and other materials. They have an extensive music collection which includes Bluegrass, Old-Time Vocal, American Vernacular Dance, and Early Country Music specific to the region. Their archives also include intriguing documentation of subcultures in the region, such as the "Helvetia" community, descendants of Swiss farmers that migrated to central West Virginia in the mid 1800s; this collection includes videotaped interviews from the 1990s that document the history, culture, and folk life of the Helvetia community.

Unfortunately, preserving audiovisual materials comes with challenges, "tapes lose their magnetism, video recordings quickly deteriorate, and digital media like DVDs can be scratched beyond play if not stored properly."[85] In 2015, Davis & Elkins sought and received assistance from the National Endowment for Humanities (NEH) to improve their preservation efforts and processes. Programs such as the NEH are an integral part of keeping preservation viable in communities that cannot afford state of the art facilities and technology. For more than twenty years the NEH has been awarding Preservation Assistance Grants to a number of institutions across the country to support and protect valuable humanities collections.[86]

Education is essential to continuing the preservation of Appalachian heritage and culture. Recognizing more heritage sites in the area, allows for locals to learn more about the area's history in a way that they will be able to have a more intimate connection with. Implementing talking tours and interactive museums at these sites can make these sites and their history have a more lasting impression on visitors. Examples of interactive learning opportunities include festivals celebrating different cultures that have blended in the region such as German, Scots-Irish, and Swiss, workshops on canning your own vegetables safely or quilt making, and academic conferences highlighting hot topic issues in the region. With the heavy use of social media, there is also an opportunity to connect with people virtually and expand their knowledge of Appalachian heritage from the comfort of their living room or commute to work with podcasts, video tours, E-flyers, and virtual workshops.

Educating those in Appalachian communities about the importance of their heritage can help deter the shame many Appalachians' feel about where they come from. I previously mentioned the "internal colony" model, which some educators in the region are embracing to help give the youth of the region a better understanding of the region's exploitation.[87] Ada Smith, the founder of the Stay Together Appalachia Youth Project, gave her perspective of the model:

> [It] allowed me to understand that my people, my heritage, and culture were not the problem, and gave me a way in which I could more easily understand power… This in turn connected me to issues around racism, classism, and homophobia because of their structural nature.[88]

By teaching students about the true nature the rest of the nation has played a role in their communities, it can empower them to help and serve their communities, in addition to showing them the value of their heritage.

When Appalachians see the worth in their communities, they may stay in the region. Some may question the consequence of native Appalachians leaving their hometowns, but what people fail to realize is that when all of the natives that were able to get a college degree and flee the area it leaves a lack of doctors, educators, and other valuable professionals. Sequentially, this creates a cycle of lack of resources for small rural communities scattered all across Appalachia. It is equally important to educate those outside of the region about the contributions Appalachians have made as well as the significance of Appalachian heritage. When people understand the triumphs and tribulations of Appalachia, it may break down many of the stereotypes and misconceptions they have held. Educating the public about Appalachia could lead to advocacy for the region, more becoming narratives in the media, and a genuine appreciation of Appalachian culture. Lastly, education is the key to destroying the relationship between the rest of the United States and the "otherness" of Appalachia. Imagine a world where we value Harlan County's history as much as Boston's, Charleston's, or San Francisco's.

With the resources we have today, there should not be a reason for Appalachian heritage to diminish. We have the ability to preserve Egyptian tombs, dinosaur bones, and scraps of papers belonging to our Founding Fathers, so we should be able to preserve video interviews from the 1990s pertaining to Appalachian history. The difference between what we see in the Smithsonian and what sits in archives at Davis & Elkins College is that the Smithsonian has more federal and public support. Community engagement and support can make a difference, but federal funding for preservation efforts in Appalachian communities is a necessity (Figure 1.1).

Figure 1.1: An example monument to the preservation of Appalachian heritage, the West Virginia Coal Miner statue by sculptor Burl Jones, completed in 2002 at the state capitol in Charleston, West Virginia. West Virginia Collection within the Carol M. Highsmith Archive, Library of Congress, Prints and Photographs Division.

## Chapter 2: From Farming to Forestry

By Chris Cone

Today, few of my family members own farmland and the ones that do are very distant. The land is no longer handed down, but the traditions born from agriculture remain, thus making the pursuit of place entirely relatable. For my ancestors, each sought their own version of the American dream. For one side of my family, it was their search for land, and the opportunities that came with it that led them to settle in Georgia and South Carolina. The value that land had for my ancestors, and the eventual disappearance of it within my own lifetime will be examined within this chapter. I will introduce prominent family members that can speak to the different types of farming, and from there, discuss how various family branches lost the land that meant so much. The importance of their cultural heritage will also be presented. The traditions my grandparents instilled, having learned from their grandparents, still remain in some fashion. Despite the loss of land, the cultural heritage is there. From the continuance of my family's heritage to the documentation and research of the past, there exists themes of preservation that will be conveyed. Each aspect provides a layered and descriptive narrative of where I come from and how it continues unto today.

The Flynns, my mother's paternal family, were tenant farmers. They did not own land, but worked it as their own, paying portions of their crops or cash to the owner. Their location would change as their circumstances did, passing through parts of Georgia. For almost a century, the Flynns worked toward success in farming. This dream was forfeited in the twentieth century as their own aspirations shifted, leaving the Flynns scattered across the Lowcountry, yet also taking their experiences with them.

The Owenbys, my mother's maternal family, were also farmers. More secure in the role, they did not need to travel for land or work for some family members owned the land they cultivated. There was less risk and certainly more stability than the latter. A diversity of crops and livestock assisted them economically, allowing for outsourced labor that consisted of local farmers. This benefited the community and allowed for social relationships to form. As I'll discuss later in more depth, the Flynns and the Owenbys had such a relationship. Regardless of their success, the Owenbys did not retain their homestead. For reasons unknown to me, it no longer exists; however, the memories withstand.

The Cones, my father's paternal family in South Carolina, differed from those in Georgia. They acquired more land than the Flynns or the Owenbys with varying degrees of crops and livestock but utilized the system of slavery to assist in production. As times changed, so did their practices. The Cones began to enter the world of sharecropping with former enslaved people, creating entire new dynamics while trying to retain some sense of the original socio-economic framework. These contracts allowed for freemen to work the farms as their own while still being under the authority of the former master. All three families started from an initial search for land and opportunity, and each one would lose it in the end.

**What Does Land Mean?**

In today's world, land is thought of in terms of real estate, a physical landscape that can be bought and sold for the purpose of housing or at times, making a profit. The traditional, European mindset valued land for its monetary value, and authority that would follow. This value system continued into the Americas, as the prospect of owning land was a very real one due to the removal and relocation of Native Americans. Land brought opportunity, food sources, shelter, community, and economic potential. It also had very real social, religious, and cultural aspects that made it significant.

Early settlers depended upon the land, and the workforce to cultivate it for them to survive. To understand my ancestors' involvement with land and what it meant to them, the five senses of quality communities will be examined. Sense of place, sense of identity, sense of evolution, sense of ownership, and sense of community are all shown below. Each of these senses distinguish something significant that land brought with it, applying both to the past and the present.

1. **Sense of Place**: Both the built and natural environment should be used to express the particularity of this place. That this community is neither "anyplace" nor "no place" but "someplace," unduplicated anywhere else.

❖ A sense of place is the attachment to the built and natural environment that surrounds them, and the key qualities that each individual associates and deems important that differentiate it from any other setting. For the Flynns, the movement from each place could have signaled something significant that embodied this principle. They were in search of something that they could belong to and could belong to them. This could apply to any of my family members because they each found themselves attempting to build a life for their family in the world of agriculture.

2. **Sense of Identity**: In economics it is the differentiated product that commands a financial premium. A community which in the long term wants to be a "valuable place", however that is defined, needs to identify its attributes that differentiate it from anywhere else.

❖ A sense of identity is all about knowing who you are, and what you're providing to the communities. Each family member would have identified as a farmer or skilled tradesman, but that is not the only identity that they belonged to. Within this sense exists many possibilities for someone to associate with something that separates them from the other. For the Owenbys, their sense of identity was much more realized. Family members who owned land and were fairly successful in the production of their crops, had this success as part of their identity. Like the Flynns, their sense of place was connected to the space that they inhabited, but it went beyond simply occupying it. It was a place to thrive.

3. **Sense of Evolution**: Successful, living communities will neither be frozen in time as museum relics nor look like they were built yesterday. The physical fabric of a community reflects its functional, cultural, aesthetic and historical evolution.

❖ A sense of evolution is about evolving with the times, and not being stuck in the past. This is the hardest of the five senses to catalog when referencing my ancestry. I don't know the particulars of the places and physical features of the buildings or towns they occupied, but I believe that this applies most to the Cone and the Flynn families, but for different reasons. The Cones were enslavers, and when they could no longer be, they went into the sharecropping business. They set up contracts that gave portions of land to the formerly enslaved people. This would have benefited the Cones, as they would have likely taken a cut of the crops and/or wages made, plus it would have allowed for a more modern sense of slavery. The tenants were mandated by the doctrines of the contract, and any delineation from it could have forfeited the tenant's access to the land and opportunity. This was an unfortunate fact about my family. Eventually, the Cones would find themselves no longer farming, as would the majority of family members. This could have been due to decline in business, but also, a desire by the next generation to do something else. By the 1930s, the Flynns slowly retreated from the occupation, and found new opportunities. Sometimes evolution is not just about how we evolve, but how land use evolves too. The lands that once belonged to my family have all changed in some way.

4. **Sense of Ownership**: If there needs to be responsibility exercised at the local level to create and benefit from economic health, then there has to be a sense of individual stake arising from that place and fellow citizens.

❖ A sense of ownership is about having something to call your own, to be responsible for it, and to maintain it for the future. Each family would have had this goal in mind, but only the Cone family and some Owenby family members were able to attain it. While not all owned property, each person could own what they were able to acquire and have pride in that.

5. **Sense of Community**: A sense of community acknowledges the obligations to and interconnectedness with other residents of that place.

❖ With a sense of community, there is an understanding of what the community can bring for you, but also, what you can do for the community. When I picture the Owenby and Flynn families, I imagine the ideals of community, as they both depended on and benefited from each other. The Flynns received money for labor on the farm, and the Owenbys were able to acquire the additional manpower. This was common practice for neighboring farmers too. For the Cone family, they provided services that assisted the community outside of farming. They used their tradesmen skills (blacksmithing and wheelwright) to earn extra money, and through those skills developed relationships with people within the area.

Each one of these senses applies to my family. Land and opportunity at something better beyond surviving and having a place to work and live on. Not all succeeded in every aspect, but each had a sense of ownership, was part of a community that they depended on, a place to belong, and an evolution for themselves and the land they worked on as part of their identity.

**Literature Review:**

This section covers the basic historical understanding and context behind agriculture in the Lowcountry. The major sources used cover plantation overseers in South Carolina, images and the history of Marietta, Georgia; agriculture in Cobb County, Georgia; rural life in the Lowcountry, the pattern of migration and settlement in South Carolina, sharecropping, urban expansion and the loss of farmland, and the labor used for agriculture until World War I. These pieces of information serve to aid in the overall narrative of how my family became farmers and the reasons they departed from the profession.

***Masters of Violence: The Plantation Overseers of Eighteenth-Century Virginia, South Carolina, and Georgia – by Tristan Stubbs:*** This text examines the shift from the popular opinions of the eighteenth century to the negative views of the latter nineteenth century on the profession of overseer, which is defined as a person who supervises others. Historically, an overseer was in charge of running the plantation, and maximizing profits by producing high yield crops, and controlling the workforce (slaves), often times with violence. It gives insight into this by examining newspapers, diaries, plantation records, and other available materials. This information will help aid an understanding, and allow for context toward a profession that at least one of my ancestors was involved in.

***Marietta: Images of America, 1833-2000 – by James Bolan Glover V, Joe McTyre, and Rebecca Nash Paden:*** The images within Marietta provide an overview that the city played within Georgia, as well as its growth from the Old South to 2000. It is broken into numerous time periods, showcasing each in its significance with prominent individuals, places, and monuments. The agricultural photos highlight a moment in time that speak to my own ancestry, seeing a day in the life of a Georgia farmer. The introduction of Lockheed Martin Aeronautics is especially important, as it affected the trajectory of the city, providing technological innovations and new opportunities for many residents. My grandfather opted to pursue employment with this company, leaving behind the life of a farmer. Here, I can better understand the transition from farmer to mechanical engineer.

***Cobb County: Images of America – by Rebecca Nash Paden and Joe McTyre:*** This book provides an understanding of life within Cobb County, covering significant people, places, and monuments. My grandparents grew up in rural Cobb County, where their parents worked the farms, a profession that went back for many generations. Both my grandmother and grandfather worked alongside their parents, as it was their livelihood. This text gives a brief introduction into the specific towns that my grandparents inhabited such as Marietta, and Kennesaw, and by accessing these images, it will give a more complete picture as to what their lives might have looked like.

***Rural Life in the Lowcountry of South Carolina: Images of America – by Dennis S. Taylor:*** Rural life in the Lowcountry takes imagery from the early twentieth century that looks at the everyday citizen in the agricultural and working class field to highlight how necessary, but also challenging it was to survive. These areas ranged from tending crops, to curing meats, and trading livestock, as well as home demonstrations that incorporated the functional re-use of upholstery, sewing, and skilled crafts that could be used in the home. The landscape is of great importance through the associated architecture that evolved as time progressed. From this book, I can see correlations with my family, who were in the agriculture business throughout parts of the Lowcountry, and better appreciate where I come from.

***Sharecropping in History and Theory – by Joseph D. Reid, Jr.:*** The article details the facts behind what a tenant farmer or sharecropper might have had to deal with, what types of crops they were expected to produce, and the surplus, as well as the conditions from the owner of the land that the tenants rented. It was my understanding that my family owned their land, and while some did, this was not true for all. This book allows me to understand the rules and regulations that were set upon the tenant farmer, and how closely that might relate to my family. Additionally, it provides reasons as to the departure from this lifestyle for my ancestors, especially when the system was arduous.

The research methods used consisted primarily of primary and secondary sources that gave insight into the types of crops that my family grew, and the areas that they inhabited. The secondary sources contributed to the overall history and understanding of the places in which they lived. Additionally, oral interviews were conducted to allow for first-hand knowledge of the people and places of interest to be expressed. The limitations experienced were that there were fewer family members that remember this history, so pieces of the puzzle remain. Online documents only provide so much of the story, therefore there exists great gaps in the narrative.

**My Cultural Experience:**

I'm from Knightsville, South Carolina, a small town outside of Summerville that was primarily rural growing up, but today is more developed. It had one corner store that served as a convenience store, gas station, and coin laundromat. My grandfather, Murray Cone, or "Papa," frequented that spot for breakfast and a game of checkers with friends, likely a tradition he had grown into. It was the kind of place where you walked inside and immediately knew everyone there because they had been there each and every day, and they knew you too. You can't escape that reality in a small town. The store has since been lost, replaced by Walgreens and CVS across the way, as well as the small town feel that once inhabited the space. It was a rural place that I could not appreciate because I could not relate to it. I did not understand its value. I only saw what it was lacking urban amenities. As I've grown older, and lost those that I love, I've begun to appreciate where they came from. I can see what they tried to teach me, as it was taught to them. I can recognize an intangible culture that was unfamiliar to me before, and the traditions that have been neglected. These places may be forgotten to many, and the landscape changed, but the desire to connect to my rural roots is steadfast.

My grandmother, Barbara Owenby Flynn never discussed her parents or where she came from. I never knew that she grew up on a farm, but it was very apparent looking back on her now. I remember her affinity for plants. She had a garden at the back of her house, and the porch was covered in hanging plants. I don't remember all the things that she grew, but tomatoes stick out the most for me. She would wrap them in caged wire holders to provide support, and protection to ensure they matured. As a child, I would mimic these actions, enlisting my grandmother's assistance in my own garden. I opted for herbs and flowers rather than vegetables, as they were less dependent upon me to survive. I was only a child, and my green thumb was barely green at all. Her marriage of skill and knowledge aided me, but never fully formed within my own endeavors. I am not now, nor will I ever likely be a professional at gardening, but I value those past moments and understand the reality of what was happening, that she was planting those seeds of knowledge (pun intended) much like what had been done for her and those before her. This cultural heritage fosters traditions that stay with us. Through these traditions we honor her memory.

My dad's family comes from Walterboro, Harleyville, and Summerville, South Carolina; all fairly rural. My grandparents lived on Highway 61, in Summerville. It was a decent lot next to a small farm and a watch tower. The tower was a part of the South Carolina Forestry Commission, where Mama would work, ensuring that no forest fires had a chance to start. She'd direct my Papa to grab the tractor and put out the fires. When they weren't protecting Summerville, they were working in their yard. I remember the little farm that sat next to the house. It was 100 feet wide by 100 feet in length with fifteen or so horizontal trenches. Every other row had a different fruit or vegetable though the majority consisted of cabbage, greens, carrots, and corn. My cousins and I learned how to plant the crops, but honestly, I remember picking the fruits and vegetables more than I do planting them. We were little and just enjoyed the time outside with them because we got to eat what we picked. Papa's shed stored the remaining food for later. While just a shed, it was a very social space where the family came together, and I have many memories from that little run down shack. I didn't realize what they were teaching us. Things that their parents had taught them, so I value that time, especially because this place is lost to us, existing only in memory.

As I got older, other familiar places began to disappear, and the traditions that went with it. My Uncle Freddie had owned a cattle ranch in Knightsville. It was something that the whole family enjoyed. My father and I would fish on the creek at the back of the ranch. It's a good memory of the two of us because I rarely enjoyed the "country" things that my father loved. Freddie eventually sold the ranch, allowing the land to be turned into a subdivision, changing the entire landscape. This moment is interesting to me, as it marks a time where transition appeared. I can remember the farm, and how that was a part of our family life, and then it was gone. It was no longer a part of our lives. I couldn't hop the fence and run to the creek. I couldn't interact with the animals because they were no longer there, and family functions there were just a distant memory.

My father purchased a small portion of land not far from the ranch and created a space for his family. The development sits directly across the fence, so it's always there, ever present of the change it created for us. The farm may have died out, but the farming did not. Papa tends to his own little garden each day, and I know I can learn a few things from him now that I appreciate it more as an adult. Through these relationships, and continued practices, the cultural heritage lives on despite the loss of land. Knightsville is certainly not the same place that it once was, but it is still my home, and I will remember it.

**Marietta & Cobb County: The History of Home**

My mother's side of the family is broken down into two sides, the Flynns and the Owenbys. Within, I'll be discussing the Flynn family, beginning with my 3rd great-grandfather, the earliest person that I am able to identify. I have provided a brief history of the Cobb County area consisting mostly of Marietta, but Kennesaw is another portion that was called home. Cobb County, Georgia was inhabited by the Creek and Cherokee peoples when the European settlers arrived in the area in the early nineteenth century. It was widely pristine with massive forests, Native American settlements, and ample supplies of land.

Almost a decade later, the entire landscape had been transformed by schoolhouses, railroads, economic trade posts, industrial development, churches, and farms. By the 1820s, settlers from the Carolinas, Alabama, and other parts of Georgia began occupying Native American territory, as it was home to clear, freshwater streams, and opportunity. The American settlements were founded in 1832, but to do this, the Cherokees that were inhabiting the land had to be moved off of it. In 1831, Georgia sought to acquire Cherokee land, organizing all territory west of the Chattahoochee River and north of Carroll County be combined into one massive county, called Cherokee. Whites were now allowed to settle and occupy the former Cherokee towns. Between 1838 and 1840, over 15,000 Native Americans from Georgia, North Carolina, Tennessee, and Alabama were relocated off of their homelands to Oklahoma, called the Trail of Tears.

## The Flynn & Owenby Families: Tenant Farmers

### Thomas Micajah Cage Flynn

Thomas Micajah "Cage" Flynn was born in 1831 in Upson, Georgia. It is otherwise referred to as Upson County located in the west central Piedmont portion of Georgia. Thomas' life prior to marriage is relatively unknown. It is assumed that he was a tenant farmer, as each succeeding relative was, but it cannot be confirmed. There are no documents that speak to those early years outside of the marriage certificate between Thomas Flynn and Sarah Kennedy, dated 1852. Sarah would pass two years later, cause unknown, and Thomas would remarry that same year. In 1854, Thomas married Sarah Ann Arrington, and they had six children.[1] By 1860, he owned no real estate, but had a personal estate worth $150.[2] This personal estate does not account for land, but does include clothing, furniture, cash, tools, livestock, and enslaved people.

There are no records of enslaving for Thomas or his family, but it cannot be dismissed entirely for Thomas had direct involvement in slavery through his role as an overseer in Upson. Within the plantation system, an overseer would work directly under the master of the estate, driving his demands for productivity by forcing the enslaved workforce into submission through violent and oppressive means. This meant that he would have controlled and supervised enslaved people toward the production of profitable crops like sea island cotton and rice, both staples for the southern states. There was likely some influence from his father-in-law, Peter Arrington, who worked as an overseer in Thomaston, Georgia.[3]

Thomaston is a prime example of a place that might have employed Thomas due to its many plantations, factories, and mills as well as its associations with the Arrington family. It sits directly in the middle of Upson County and was incorporated in 1825. It was founded by numerous settlers from eastern counties of Georgia, portions of North Carolina, South Carolina, and New England. Its claim to fame was textiles, as Upson had four textile mills prior to the Civil War, positioning it as the leader in the industry. Additionally, by 1860, Upson County had an expanding population of over 10,000 people with the number of Black and whites almost equal.[4] Thomas' residence was Georgia Militia District 589 otherwise known as Hootenville, which no longer exists.[5] It was originally named Blountsville after John Blount, but a post office in another county had the same name, so to deter confusion the decision was made to change the name of the town when large areas of the land was purchased by Henry Hooten.

Hootenville sat within the southeastern portion of Upson County, roughly making up ten percent of it. It was ripe with farmland, crepe myrtles, fig trees, and a bustling little town center that housed a hotel, a few barrooms, a grocery and general store, and a blacksmith shop. Traditionally it served as a relay and way station for travelers coming from Macon, Georgia where the horses and stagecoaches could be maintained, and people could find refreshments. By the 1860s, the decline of Hootenville began to set in with the majority of employers relocating to Thomaston. Hootenville claimed only a handful of shops and residents within its district, dying out towards the early twentieth century.[6]

On October 20, 1863, Thomas enlisted in the 46th Infantry, serving as a private for the Confederacy.[7] This regiment was referred to as the "Upson Sentinels", consisting of soldiers from Upson, Schley, Harris, Muscogee, Chattahoochee, Webster, Marion, and Talbot counties.[8] Thomas would join his unit through Georgia, South Carolina, Mississippi, Tennessee, and North Carolina before dying of disease on July 3, 1864, in Madison, Georgia.[9] By 1870, Sarah Flynn, widow of Thomas Flynn was likely living with or nearby her family in Thomaston for Sarah and her children are shown directly underneath them in the 1870 US Census.[10] The decline of Hootenville, and the death of her husband were plausible factors that could have prompted her move to Thomaston. Being close to her family, having additional support, and a place for her children is an image that is easily conjured.

**James D. Flynn:**

My 2nd great-grandfather, James D. Flynn was born in 1855, and was the oldest of his siblings. After his father's death, he likely filled the void as best he could, being only 9 years old. When his family relocated to the Thomaston area, he would have had much influence from his uncles on how to maintain and run a farm, as they were farm hands. Tenant farming is assumed, but unclear. In 1880, James Flynn and his brother William Flynn are recorded as general farmers in the US Census, residing and renting in Kennesaw, Georgia with his mother, aunt, and sister.[11] It is the first account of tenant farming within the Flynn family. There are no records of what James planted, and harvested, but it can easily be theorized based on what was in demand for the area at that time for that region, which was cotton. In October 1880, James married Arminda J. Kirk, and they had four children. Arminda passed in 1892 from complications from childbirth, as her son William Burdine Flynn was born that same year. In February 1893, James then married Rebecca Hudgens.[12]

By 1900, James is recorded as a farmer, residing, and renting the property in Oregon, Cobb County, Georgia, which is near Marietta.[13] Again, no agricultural schedules could be found, but the usual suspects of cotton, apples, peaches, corn, and livestock are likely candidates. It appears that every decade or so James picked up and relocated from one place to the next. Beginning in Hootenville as a child, then to Thomaston, followed by Kennesaw, and lastly Oregon. The journey from Thomaston to Kennesaw would have been a lengthy one, as the trip is just under 100 miles. He didn't own the land he worked on, so it might have been easier to pick up and travel to where the work was offered. My Aunt Pam refers to the Flynn family as "poorer than poor," so there was always this sort of stigma attached to the Flynn name.[14] There could be a fresh start with each new place, attempting to brush off previous failures and/or associations. From this point until his death in the 1930s, where no official death certificate exists, there is no mention of James. He completely disappears from the records, leaving questions that cannot be answered. His children would; however, continue in his footsteps.

**Lucious Leethaniel Flynn:**

Lucious Leethaniel Flynn, my great-grandfather, was born on April 5, 1886.[15] He was a tenant farmer like his father before him though no records exist to validate this prior to 1930. There are a lot of unknowns, but I would expect him to pick up these trades since it was something that was done by numerous members of his family on both sides, plus the area that he was living in was mostly surrounded by farms and open fields. By 1910, he worked as a farm laborer for the Gray family in Kennesaw.[16] It is plausible that this could have been an additional job on top of his tenant farming. As mentioned earlier, the Flynns were fairly poor compared to other neighboring families, according to my aunt. This additional labor may have been necessary to make ends meet. It is likely that this was not the first time the Flynns entered into these agreements, having to find alternative means to help the family out in whatever capacity was available to them. It certainly would not be the last, considering that Luther, Lucious's son, would later go on to work for the Owenby family while also helping his father maintain their own farm.[17]

According to this account, Joseph and Porter Owenby in Union County, relatives of the Owenbys in Cobb County that employed Luther, owned between 20 to 500 acres of land that contained such crops as wheat, rye, Indian corn, oats, and tobacco. Additionally, the livestock included horses, oxen, cows, sheep, and pigs.[18] By 1918, Lucious was a farmer residing in Marietta, Georgia according to his World War I draft registration card.[19] It does not list him as a tenant farmer, but the word "farmer" is used to describe him.

By the 1930s, he is shown as a general farmer, residing and renting the property in Marietta.[20] This is the first document that shows his rental status on the farm, highlighting that he worked as a farmer, but did not own the land. Lucious did not stay on the farm long after due to a heart condition. He had little to no support from his family by this time, as his son chose another field of work altogether.[21] By the 1940s, the family had relocated to Kennesaw where Lucious's daughter, Gertrude, took on the role of helping her father. She put herself through cosmetology school and opened up a small salon in the area. It had to have been difficult to leave the farm life behind, but it was no longer possible to live that lifestyle. Lucious passed away on February 7, 1945. Parts of the farm still exist today, but it is no longer used as a farm. Instead, it operates as an open airfield for the Cobb County International Airport.

**Luther Leethaniel Flynn:**

Luther was born on July 13, 1925, in rural Kennesaw, Georgia.[22] His relationship with farming was more strained than other relatives. His home life was a stressful one, having to help his father on their farm, but also, work as a farm laborer for the Owenby family. As mentioned previously, the Owenbys employed Luther in the Cobb County area. He found this line of work at a young age, being only 9 when he began. This is how he met my grandmother, Barbara Owenby. I have two photos of them around that age. Luther presents with a goofy grin, and my grandmother matches his energy and smile. It was apparent she liked him even back then though she had more in common with Luther than just their affection for one another. She was ready for something else apart from the farm life that they were both used to, and so was Luther. My Aunt Pam said he never took to farm life, only doing it because he had to. It was something his father expected of him, and his father before him, so the first chance he got, he found an alternative. She believes that Lucious was a tough man to have as a father, possibly abusive since Luther left as soon as he was able to.[23]

When Luther was 15, he registered for the draft, readying himself to leave it all behind. Additionally, on the card, the occupation of Luther and Lucious was written as tenant farmer, which had never been stated before, only assumed from the rental status in other documents.[24] He enlisted in the U.S. Marine Corps Reserves in 1943, serving as a Corporal by the end of his term in 1946.[25] After returning home, Luther took a job as an aircraft mechanic for Lockheed Martin Corporation. He was employed there for over a decade but was let go due to alcoholism. The war had left him with many psychological issues, and Luther opted to drink those problems away.[26] He relocated his family to Summerville and worked as a sheet metalsmith until his death in 1967.[27] There is more to his story, but my family has asked me not to speak on it, so I am respecting their wishes. My family does not talk about my grandfather because of his alcoholism. I grew up never knowing anything about him or the life he lived. He is perhaps the primary reason as to why the Flynns no longer work or reside on the farm. It appears that attitudes shifted in the twentieth century for my family, and that life on the land did not hold up to the version of what their ancestors had hoped for. Luther had the option to try something different, and as a result life in Summerville became my home.

**James Arrington Owenby:**

James Arrington Owenby was born in Cobb County on February 6, 1886. He came from a big family that spread across the midlands of Georgia and into

North Carolina. James was one of nine children, and his father was one of twelve. He married Ola King in 1908 and had twelve children.[28] They were farmers like the Flynns but were more successful in their endeavors.

Until recently, I had believed the Owenbys owned their farm, but according to census documents, this was not the case. By 1920, James is recorded as a general farmer and renting the residence.[29] This contradicts the oral statements made by my family members; however, I do understand how this can be misconstrued. As seen earlier in the agricultural schedule, James' uncles, Joseph and Porter Owenby owned their lands. Thus, some members of the Owenby family owned land while others did not.

According to the 1910 census, John Owenby, James's father, owned land.[30] As to what happened after this, it is unknown. Perhaps it was lost or was handed down to one of James' siblings. An additional possibility is that James rented land from his family. What is known though is that each decade James is shown as a tenant farmer with the latest entry confirming this in 1940.[31] My Aunt Pam distinctly remembers fields of apple trees on her grandbudgie's farm. She called him grandbudgie because his nickname was Bud. My mother remembers the apple and peach trees along with corn. They differed on what they grew but remember their grandparents fondly. James passed away in 1972, and the farm no longer survives to my family's knowledge.[32]

**The Cone Family: From Farming to Forestry**

I had never known that my family was so entrenched in the life of farming, and that each of my grandparents had lived that life. I can see how it has carried over into their gardening, and the memories that I carry from my childhood, but aside from that, we seem to be separated from it. I was able to uncover information on the land that my ancestors owned, and the question nagged at me, where did it all go? With the aid of my father and grandfather, I was able to fill in those gaps, and provide a more complete picture of the Cone family. I begin with Adam Miles Cone, my paternal 3rd great-grandfather, as this is the furthest that I am able to go back. From what I can tell, farming started with him.

**Adam Miles Cone:**

Adam Miles Cone was born sometime between 1815 and 1816 in Harleyville, South Carolina. Documents differ on the date, as there is no official birth certificate. In 1836, Adam applied for a land bounty warrant that allowed him to obtain land for the purpose of farming.[33] This was a common practice from 1775 to 1855 via the government to encourage enlistment in military service by offering the land as a bounty through a warrant application process. Adam's application was approved, and a plat was commissioned on December 8, 1836, for 742 acres of land on Penny Creek in Colleton County (Figure 2.1). [34] Locating this land has been difficult, but I believe that it existed nearby Penny Creek Landing, a boat landing in the Walterboro area. There are no military records from this time to verify Adam's service aside from what the land grant dictates. He was shown as a private in the South Carolina Militia under Captain T. Fupp.[35] All attempts to locate information on his regiment have been fruitless; however, given the political climate, it is easy to theorize as to where Adam's service may have taken him.

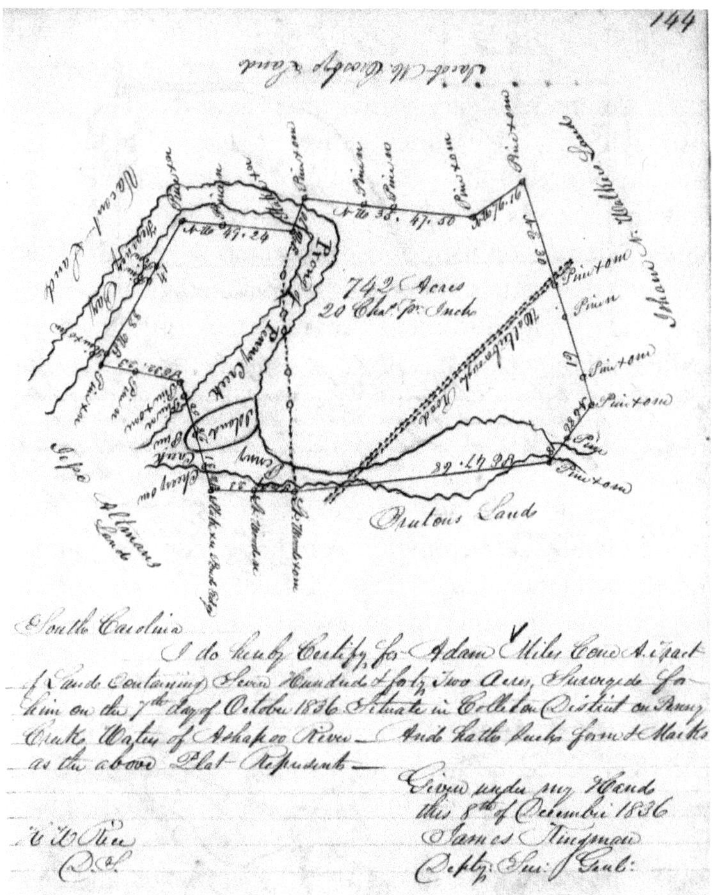


Figure 2.1: Adam Miles Cone Plat for 742 Acres on Penny Creek, Surveyed by Henry W. Rice, December 8, 1836. SC Department of Archives and History, Series: S213190, Volume: 41, Page: 144.

During this time, conflicts existed between Native Americans and white settlers. Between 1835 and 1842, the Second Seminole War was a serious concern for America and the Lowcountry. As seen in the Florida Historical Society Quarterly, "Near the end of December 1835, the citizens of Savannah, Georgia, and Charleston, South Carolina, had begun to realize the gravity of the situation in Florida."[36] Previously, in the First Seminole War (1817-1818) Florida was sold to the United States by Spain. In 1823, the Treaty of Moultrie Creek was made, which removed the Seminole people to a four million acre reservation in central Florida. The treaty also allowed for white settlers to build roads and encroach upon the reservation territory. The U.S. government was to facilitate this move; however, it was slow to deliver on its promises, prompting heated attacks between the white settlers and Seminole residents.

In 1830, President Andrew Jackson signed the Indian Removal Act, allowing for the removal and relocation of all Native Americans west of the Mississippi River. Another treaty was initiated, the Treaty of Payne's Landing in 1832 that granted the Seminoles an additional three years to fully move off of Florida land. The Seminoles were to be absorbed into the Creek settlement regardless of their opinions on the matter, and in 1833 were pressured into signing the Treaty of Fort Gibson, which essentially restated the terms of the previous treaty. The Seminoles denied having agreed to the terms of removal from their land. By 1834, Osceola, while not a chief, became the leader of the Seminole and affirmed their resistance to the move by creating an allied force against it. On December 28, 1835, the combined forces of the Seminoles and their allies attacked the troops commanded by Major Francis Dade, enroute from Fort Brooke to Fort King. Out of one hundred soldiers, only three survived. This event marked the beginning of the Second Seminole War, known as the Dade Massacre.[37]

The Seminoles continued to instill fear into the white settler, and soldiers alike with their guerilla warfare, retreating into the Everglades and destroying supply lines and outposts with every opportunity. In October 1837, Osceola was led into false pretenses under the guise of truce into St. Augustine, Florida under the command of General T.S. Jessup. He was imprisoned, and remanded to Fort Moultrie in South Carolina, where he died.[38] After the capture and death of Osceola their efforts would cease to garner much success, and in 1842, around 4,000 native peoples were moved from their home. On August 14, 1842, the war ended, and advertisements were introduced via the Armed Occupation Act that offered up portions of Seminole land for white settlement within Florida.

By 1842, Adam married Sarah Ann Willis, and had four children. In 1850, Adam's occupation was listed as a wheelwright, which is a person who makes and repairs wheels for horse drawn carriages.[39] In 1859, Sarah gave birth to their fourth child, Miles Cone, and incidentally died shortly after. After her death, Adam remarried that same year to Martha Ann Davis. There is no information that can be presented for Sarah or Martha per their home life or upbringing, as the only information about them exists as the wives of Adam Miles Cone. By 1860, Adam was shown as a farmer with an estate worth $500 in Colleton County; however, his property did not limit itself to just land.[40] He was an enslaver though for how long is unknown. Within the schedule, it showed two slave quarters, and four enslaved people that consisted of one female, and three males. No names are given, but in 1860, the female was 40 years old, and the three boys were ages 12, 7, and 5, so likely her children.[41] There is also the possibility that the three boys could have been his children too. By 1864, Adam served as a Private and blacksmith for the 11th Reserves Infantry in the Confederate Army from April to November of that year. No other information exists regarding this matter.[42] By April 1865, the Civil War was over, and a new reality without slavery set in. While Adam enslaved people, there are no documents that state any of the names; however, the same cannot be said for his son, Joseph Hamilton Cone.

In 1866, Joseph set up a contract for March Middleton that leased a portion of land to him and his heirs to hold and use, but under the authority of Joseph.[43] This is what is referred to as sharecropping, which allows the tenant to use the land in return for a portion of the crops or wages earned. Sharecropping followed these six stipulations.[44]

1. The amount of land to be sharecropped.
2. The share for each crop.
3. The land for allowed crops, including the requirements that the tenant plant all of the land and appropriately cultivate and harvest the crops.
4. Tenant and landlord payment shares for and maintenance duties with respect to cooperating inputs (such as implements, work animals, and fertilizers).
5. Responsibilities for land improvements (primarily duties relating to the maintenance and improvement of fences, hedges, irrigation ditches, fertility, and barns).
6. Penalties for noncompliance.

This allowed for Joseph and other family members to utilize this workforce to produce additional income while having to work less. As previously stated, sharecropping was the new system of slavery that would hold the worker accountable to the landowner. Any sort of straying from the contract would terminate it, resulting in the loss of land and homelessness.

By 1880, Joseph and his brother William are shown in an agricultural report that allows for an understanding of what types of crops they produced and the livestock that they had. Much of this report references the totals that they had in 1870 but is dated 1880. For Joseph, he had 150 acres of land, though only 15 acres were improved with the rest being woodlands and forests. This amounted to a worth of $500 for the land. It consisted of Indian corn, bales of cotton, cane sugar, and sweet potatoes as the primary crops. Livestock contained horses, oxen, milking cows, swine, and other types of cattle. In the same report, William had significantly more land than his brother. He owned 366 acres that was valued at $800. His crops and livestock were essentially the same with only some numbers slightly different; however, his value was much higher. From the combined total of livestock and production, his net worth was $1,390.[45] Adam had acquired a significant amount of land in the Walterboro and Summerville areas, and that he was distributing this land to his children, but very few records exist for other children outside of Joseph and William. By 1889, Adam Miles Cone passed away, and the land was left to his sons.

**John Wesley Cone:**

In 1847, John Wesley Cone was born in Colleton County, one of four children. As previously shown, two of his three brothers were involved in farming and owned land; however, no agricultural reports exist that can show what John grew and how much land he owned. By 1880, John is shown as a farmer, married to Sarah Bowers with four children in the Colleton County area.[46] It is assumed that it is his land since his brothers had their own land, but the 1880 census does not show a rental or ownership status. By 1900, the census records John as a farmer and portrays him as owning the land.[47] John died March 5, 1901. There is no death certificate, so the cause of death is unknown. John is rarely seen in documents aside from the census reports. There are no service records or newspaper articles to reference. His life was a short one, having died at age 44. As to the land that he owned, I presume that it was left to one of his other sons, and not my great-grandfather since no further records show direct family as landholders.

**John Harvey Cone:**

John Harvey Cone was born in June 1887, in Colleton County. From all the records that were found, it does not appear that John retained the land that his family had established for themselves in years prior. In 1900, he was seen as a farm laborer in the Burns-Dorchester area, which is between Walterboro and Summerville.[48] By 1910, he was residing in Georgetown, South Carolina and was listed as an apprentice. It doesn't state what he was apprenticing in, but it was likely as a saw filer.[49] Saw filers maintained the machinery for the lumber companies, ensuring that proper and safe protocols were being upheld. On June 5, 1917, John filed his World War I draft registration card, and listed his employment at E.P. Burton Lumber Company in Charleston.[50] After this point, it is said that things went sideways for John.

My grandfather insists that his father was missing in action for seven years, so when he returned home, he had no land. He says that his brothers had sold the land, and that it was the reason as to why his father lost it. My father and grandfather claim that this land amounted to around one-thousand acres, which spanned portions of Summerville, and Walterboro, and that it was bought by MeadWestvaco.[51] This may very well explain why and how I was unable to find documentation that states John as receiving this land, when I can see that other members of his family did. However, the timeline doesn't fit perfectly with the documented records. By 1920, John was married to Beulah Elizabeth Myers, and had their first child the same year. Had he been lost overseas for seven years this wouldn't have been possible according to how the dates line up. It is highly plausible that he was lost overseas after the war ended, but that the time of the incident was much less than is being told. I found no record of him being a prisoner of war, and I have filed for his military records to fill in the informational gaps, but that search is still ongoing. By 1930, John was a full time saw filer living in the Summerville area on the very same road that I live off of.[52] The census stated it as Georgetown, but it also listed it as Old Orangeburg Road, which tells me that the zoning was different during that time, incorporating parts of Summerville into Georgetown. There was no change for the next decade. John Harvey Cone died on February 8, 1948.

**Murray Cone (Papa) & Bertie Cone (Mama):**

Papa and Mama worked for the South Carolina Forestry Commission in the 1960s. In an interview with Papa Murray, he stated that he heard of the job opening from his cousin, Bud Knight, a former police chief of Summerville. Bud inquired about whether or not Mama would be able to climb the stairs of the tower every day, and Papa suggested that she could manage. Mama Bertie started the position of fire tower operator in 1964, prompting the move to 4527 Ashley River Road in Summerville. Her responsibilities were to ensure the safety of her fire wardens when on duty, and to look for forest fires. Papa Murray would take his truck and tractor and put out the fires. He said she always had a passion and urgency for the job because there were people out there that she cared about (Figure 2.2).[53]

When they both retired in the early 2000s, they moved off of the property. Today, the house and land sits abandoned. The tower was torn down and moved to the Nexton area as decoration for one of the buildings but has since been relocated. I do not know where it is. The tower was one of the first metal towers in the state, dubbed Middleton Tower. Papa remembers previous towers, but those were constructed from wood, and were not as tall. It is a shame that the location of the tower is unknown because it is valuable to South Carolina history, as very few are still in operation. As a kid it towered over me, roughly 100 feet in height. I can remember wanting to climb each step, but always being denied due to safety reasons. Mama passed away last year, so it is something that I associate with her and only now fully appreciate.

As to the land, it was sold to a development company that plans on turning it into a subdivision, called Ashton Woods. I was unable to uncover the exact deed to list the company name or previous owners because my dad and Papa stated that the land that my ancestors owned was sold to MeadWestvaco, or as it was also known, Phosphate Paper Company, and later Virginia/West Virginia Paper Company. It would have been nice to locate the deed or plat maps that showed the boundaries of the land and the purchaser. The area next to the old property has been laid out and houses have been built. Residents have begun to move in on the adjacent property, but the old house and land are practically unchanged. In every sense you could think of this land as still being theirs, and doing everything to protect it from danger, ensuring it for the future despite the lack of title. It was their job to foster the preservation of this land, like it is mine to preserve their memory.

Figure 2.2: "Mama" Bertie Cone at the fire tower. Photograph from the personal collection of the author.

## Conclusion:

When I began this journey, it was about where family land went and what happened to it. I believe that I have conveyed the possibilities for its disappearance, but also, the reasoning behind what the land meant to them. I now have a deeper understanding and appreciation for my family, especially my grandparents since two of them have already passed away. As I've said before, I will continue to honor them through keeping the traditions and heritage of farming alive that they instilled in me. I do not have a green thumb, but I will try to use it as best as I can to grow things. Papa still works in his garden, something that just comes naturally to him because he was born to do it, and I think it is something that he enjoys. I'm unsure what the future holds, but perhaps I will have my own garden in the future where I can channel this heritage. My family valued the practice, and as a researcher, my whole being wants to understand them. Either my sister or I will inherit the land that my father lives on, and both of us appreciate where we come from, so I have no doubt that it will be in good hands. The original lands may be lost, but the heritage of farming is very much alive.

# Chapter 3: Graniteville, South Carolina and the Importance of Small Town History

By Rebekah Seymour

When I think of my cultural identity, the first thing that comes to mind is a place: Graniteville, South Carolina - a small mill town founded in the nineteenth century. Two of my great-grandfathers worked at the mill, one of whom I got the chance to know personally, as well as one of my great-grandmothers. My father also worked for the mill company for a brief period. Four generations of my family, including myself, have lived in this town.

My great-grandfather's mill house is still standing and was only just recently sold outside the family. I remember visiting this house often as a child, and the Oatmeal Cream Pies my great-grandfather always kept in his pantry. This small town has been the setting for much of my life; and I have fond memories from my childhood about it. However, when I first tried to put into words why this place matters to my cultural history, I struggled. How do I explain to outsiders why this small town is so special to me? Many of my family lived most of their lives there, and I can see how the culture of this town is still touching my life today. The task I have set is to prove that this small town is special and explain why this should matter even to those who do not have personal ties to Graniteville.

Small towns are rarely thought of as interesting. Most people think words such as boring, sleepy, or uneventful are better suited to describe these places. Unfortunately, this means that they can be easily overlooked regarding their historical significance unless there was an event there that affected regional history on a national scale. Graniteville has received some acknowledgment due to the historical significance their progressive mill had in the mill industry in the South.

However, the mill, along with other historic buildings significant to Graniteville's history, are deteriorating. Although this small town had a large impact in the South, Graniteville's history is not being preserved as well as I believe it could be.

For generations, people worked and lived in Graniteville. The mill's walls not only supported a new form of industry in the South, but a way of life for many Americans. Graniteville's history has been examined from the viewpoint of its significance to the American South as a whole, but I want to examine why it was important to the average person who lived there. I will explain the significance of this town and its mills from the perspective of my great-grandparents and grandparents. After all, the history of the average person is as important as those who were in prominent positions. Studying history in this way requires that more perspectives are included and examined, even if that viewpoint is not very grand.

Graniteville's historic structures are slowly deteriorating due to a lack of interest or concern for the small town's past. The impact that small towns have on people is still significant, regardless of how widespread that impact may be. This will be explored as I describe the experiences of my two great-grandfathers and grandfather, which will portray the significance of this town to them, and by extension, me. I will explain how the history of Graniteville can be tied to the beginning of Southern manufacturing, an improving education system in the South, and a larger Utopian social movement in response to industrialization. Southern mill town culture is unique and is important because it is one of the many cultures that contribute to the United States; and therefore, deserves to be explored. If this small town has such a significance to American history, then it is probable that other small towns have contributions to history that have yet to be discovered.

**Literature Review**

Graniteville began with the unique founding of the town's mill, which the community was built around. The mill that started it all sits near the town's center, which is deteriorating. The Graniteville's history is personal to me because of my roots that come from there. Therefore, the lack of attention afforded to the mill's preservation also concerns me. Many historians who have studied Southern industry claim that Graniteville Mill helped start the cotton mill boom in the South after its founding in 1845. [1] Previously, many white Southerners strongly opposed the introduction of an industrial textile industry in the South.

Plantation enslavers feared that large influxes of wage laborers would not care about preserving the practice of slavery and the delicate social hierarchy in the South. Additionally, most manufacturing centers were originally located in the North, where abolitionists were more common. This caused Southerners to believe manufacturing would breed abolitionists, further encouraging planter fear of manufacturing. Very few Southerners in the 1840s were advocating for manufacturing to grow in the South, but those who did emphasized that they did not want their manufacturing system to mirror manufacturing in the North. These few advocates only wanted to diminish the South's reliance on the North. Simply the act of bringing industry to the South was unique, because textile mills in the South were rare and, at first, undesired by Southerners. This gives Graniteville significance to the history of the textile industry in the South. Tim Downey's "Riparian Rights and Manufacturing in Antebellum South Carolina: William Gregg and the Origins of the 'Industrial Mind'" describes William Gregg as a leader in the movement to bring textile mills to the South, which he initiated in Graniteville. [2] Despite this significance, the Graniteville Mill and other buildings are not being taken care of very well.

Broadus Mitchell's *William Gregg: Factory Master of the Old South* provides information on William Gregg, the founder of Graniteville Company and the town of Graniteville. This book describes how the labor source for Graniteville Company was unusual. Although most employers used enslaved people for large work projects in the South at this time, Gregg only hired poor whites. Despite enslaved labor being cheaper, he hoped to improve the lives of poor whites in the South by providing employment and founding a town that had what he believed to be a higher quality of life.[3] This is another example of how Graniteville is exceptional.

Besides the few sources previously mentioned, most of the scholarly sources concerning Graniteville only deal with the chlorine spill that resulted from a train derailment in 2005. Sixty tons of chlorine gas was spilled on the grounds of the Graniteville textile mill while 180 employees were working the night shift. These sources primarily focus on the health and environmental issues related to the accident, as well as evacuation protocols. Unfortunately, there is a lack of academic writing about Graniteville itself. This source gives a description of the disaster and the health repercussions that many town residents faced.[4] While this incident was an important chapter in the history of Graniteville, it is only a small part of its history and does not define the culture of the town.

Nathaniel Walker's *Victorian Visions of Suburban Utopia: Abandoning Babylon* discusses the nineteenth century movement to create Utopia that began in response to the Industrial Revolution. Cities were in poor condition at this time because of the large quantity of people living near the factories at which they worked. Walker's description of A.W. Pugin and Robert Owens, two men who were part of this anti-industrialization movement, explains that they wrote about various ways to improve society and create utopias in the 1840s.[5] These writings were published only a few years before William Gregg founded Graniteville, and that they, along with the movement they represented, influenced Gregg's decisions at the founding of Graniteville.

Ophélie Siméon's *Robert Owen's Experiment at New Lanark: From Paternalism to Socialism* discusses Owen's attempt to put his ideals into practice. Siméon gives an in-depth description of New Lanark and the various social practices he tried to instill there. This book demonstrates that Owen's industrial town, New Lanark, has similarities to Graniteville, which illustrate his influence on Gregg. Siméon discusses how Owen emphasized education for the children of New Lanark at a time when this was uncommon for the working class, even outside of a small-town setting.[6] His insistence on providing education is similar to Gregg's enthusiasm for education instilled in Graniteville at its founding. Siméon explains that Owen built various public spaces for the community at New Lanark in 1809.[7]

It is important to note that Owen was known throughout the world, as his increased notoriety increases the likelihood that he influenced Gregg. Donald F. Carmony and Josephine M. Elliot's *New Harmony, Indiana: Robert Owen's Seedbed for Utopia* describes Owen's purchase and move to a mill town, New Harmony, in the United States. This move allowed Owen a chance to instill his ideals in America, which further spread his ideas surrounding utopian communities. Additionally, as this move occurred in 1825, there was enough time for Owen to build his recognition in America and catch Gregg's attention.[8] This further suggests that Gregg was influenced by Owen, as Owen became widely known in America only two decades before Gregg founded Graniteville.

Timothy Mahoney in "The Small City in American History" addresses the lack of history on small towns in American history. He states that "…relatively few historians have considered the history of small towns and cities…" and instead focus on larger urban centers and how they developed. However, there are hundreds of small towns that play a role in American history. These towns have contributed to the general history of the nation because they connect are connected through industry and commerce. Yet this source focuses primarily on the history of small cities, not small towns.[9]

Miles Orvell's *The Death and Life of Mainstreet: Small towns in American Memory, Space, and Community* discusses Main Street and what it means in the American Culture. He argues that Main Street is closely associated with small towns to many Americans. The archetype associated with small towns can be partly attributed to television shows from the fifties. Orvell did not grow up in a small town, but claims he knew what living in a small town was like because of these shows. He goes on to describe Main Street as a piece of American culture, not necessarily just of small towns.[10] However, I find it interesting that a person who did not live in a small town believed they knew what it was like to live in one based off of television stereotypes. While big cities do have local neighborhood "Main Streets" that serve the community in similar fashions to smaller towns, the culture is not the same. I believe it is important to understand that not every small town in America is the same, and that they each have their own cultures and traditions that are equally as important.

Museum on Main Street is a program started by the Smithsonian to encourage small rural towns to investigate their history then share their stories and culture through pop up exhibits. This program acknowledges the importance of small-town history to American history as a whole. "The Smithsonian and state humanities councils see small towns as essential partners in documenting and understanding American history and promoting civic engagement."[11] It has also created relationships between the Smithsonian, various small-town historians, and small cultural organizations. The Smithsonian claims that there is more local support for historians' work when they are associated with the Smithsonian because local interest is peaked by the name. While the program has experimented and adjusted how they present successful exhibits, the "Smithsonian team now focuses on themes with broad general interest."[12] The program believes this produces more successful exhibits; however, it could be seen as a restrictive practice that does not give as much opportunity to focus on what local historians believe to be significant to the history of their town and its culture. Guidelines for focusing on general themes may prevent locals from presenting a unique exhibit that best portrays their small town as seen by those who live there. This is a successful program because it gives a voice to small town history so that they can contribute to the larger narrative of American history.

Karen Good's "Preservation of Small-town Character in the Town Center of Rutland, Massachusetts"[13] discusses the small-town of Rutland and how they are facing the challenge of preserving their unique culture. Good argues that many small towns in the United States are struggling to survive economically while large commercial developments threaten to replace the historical fabric that represents the town's culture. She goes on to explain how Rutland is responding to this struggle. However, the event that catapulted this action was the demolition of a Greek Revival house that had previously stood in the town center. The preservation movement in Rutland is in a sense reactive because they had to lose an important piece of their built environment before they put emphasis on preserving their history and culture. I hope that small towns will be appreciated for their contribution to history and protect their unique cultures. This is one of a few sources where a small town's history is discussed and actively preserved.

Graniteville is an example of a small town that has a few works of literature concerning the history of its mill and why it was significant to the textile industry in the South. Graniteville has also become well known amongst environmental and medical circles because of the disastrous chlorine spill that occurred there. However, the mills that caused Graniteville to be important to the textile industry are not being preserved. A whole town was built around this mill that had its own history and culture. Unfortunately, the history of many small towns in the United States are not often studied and preserved in the same way as those of large cities. Rutland, Massachusetts is an example of a small town that realized the importance of valuing and preserving its culture too late. The purpose of this paper will be to explore the culture of Graniteville through the eyes of my family and describe the state of its preservation. I hope that what I discover will capture what makes Graniteville special, and why its community should do better to preserve its past.

**Methodology**

My goal for this thesis was to explain why Graniteville is a small town with a unique culture that deserves to be preserved. I aimed to gain a greater understanding of the history of the town and what life was like living there, with my family being a case study. With four generations having lived in this town, I felt that they would be a good representation of the culture and its evolution. For this research project, I used primary and secondary sources to gain information on Graniteville and how other small towns have been tackling the issue of preservation (or lack thereof). I used the College of Charleston Library PASCAL database, Google Scholar, and the Aiken County Historical Society Archive to find my sources. I searched for anything that discussed Graniteville, its founder William Gregg, small towns, and other textile mill information. Keywords included "Graniteville", "Graniteville Company", "William Gregg", and "Southern textile mills". There was not much information on Graniteville available through the online databases, so I used these to contextualize how the history of small towns has been preserved and recorded over time. I looked specifically for sources that would discuss the culture and preservation of these towns. At the local archives, I searched for information that related to stories my family had told me during oral interviews. My goal was to determine what life was like for the average Graniteville resident at the time my great-grandfathers moved there, as well as when it was first founded. I could then use this understanding to describe the culture within Graniteville, how it had evolved, and how it was still affecting my family today.

I utilized the College of Charleston's Library databases to search for various secondary sources on the history of Graniteville, the textile industry in the South, and how often the history of small towns is being studied and preserved. These databases provided secondary sources that discussed the founder of the town, William Gregg, and the steps he took to build the mill and his town. I was able to determine that the town's founding was unique because of the mill and the common opinion of the textile industry within the South at the time, and the reasons supporting this argument. I was also able to find a few sources that explained a lack of focus on the history of small towns, as well as one example of scholarly research on the preservation of another small town in the United States. These sources proved helpful in determining that the history of small towns is a niche that has not been well explored or preserved. I used Google Scholar and the College of Charleston Library database in my attempt to obtain secondary sources on the history of Graniteville. However, despite what I described previously, I was able to find little on the history of the town unless it was related to the train derailment and chlorine spill that occurred in 2005. The lack of discussion about Graniteville before that disaster was surprising because the town played a large role in the history of Southern textile industry.

While there were not many scholarly writings on Graniteville's history, I was able to find more information through the Aiken County Historical Museum. As Graniteville is a part of Aiken County, the town has a small room dedicated to it within the museum. They also have a vertical file in the archives that contain a variety of primary sources, which I was able to use, including newspaper articles, photographs, reports that the Society had put together for local tours in order to provide a general history of the town. Additionally, there were two small booklets that had been published by locals that contained photographs and a brief history of the town. This was helpful in gaining a better foundation for understanding the town's past.

I also used Google Scholar and the College of Charleston Library PASCAL database to find primary and secondary sources concerning the Utopian Movement formed in response to industrialization and the cities it affected. I used keywords such as "Robert Owen," "A.W. Pugin," and "Utopia" to find these sources. These sources helped to explain some of the decisions that Gregg made while founding the town. Through this, I was able to find connections between Graniteville and the larger Utopia Movement of the nineteenth century, which I could use to argue for Graniteville's significance to history.

Despite the lack of plans to repurpose the Graniteville Mill, I was able to find a couple of articles that, while several years old, portrayed the desire of locals to have the mill put to use again. An article posted by a local news channel discussed the Horse Creek Trust and their efforts to rehabilitate some of Graniteville's historic structures, specifically Hickman Hall. However, it did not indicate that any plans had been made for the Graniteville Mill.[14] Another article was published by *Preservation Magazine* that discussed the town's hope for rehabilitation. It gave a brief history of Graniteville, explained preservation efforts with Hickman Hall, and gave quotes from locals expressing dreams of repurposing the mill.[15] These two articles were the only references I was able to find that discussed possible repurposing for the Graniteville Mill. While they portray a hope for the future of the historic mill, they are several years old and have yet to bring any action to fruition.

Much of the information I collected came from oral interviews I conducted with close family members, especially my grandfather, Jim Seymour, and my great-aunt, Zell Seymour. I used stories that they told me about my family as the basis for my paper and used the additional primary and secondary sources to compare this information with the rest of the Graniteville. I was also able to visit many of the places in Graniteville I discuss. I furthered my understanding by utilizing Google Earth, the Library of Congress's digital database, and other websites to obtain images of the mill during times when I could not be physically present in Graniteville (Figure 3.1). I was able to find various themes that connect my family to the town. All of this I have used as proof that Graniteville has a rich history and a special culture that deserves to be preserved.

Figure 3.1: Graniteville Mill, Marshall Street, Graniteville, Aiken County, South Carolina. Historic American Engineering Record. Library of Congress Prints and Photographs Division.

I believe that discussing Graniteville through the perspective of my family provides a unique understanding to the town's history and culture because this method will allow for readers to understand what life was like for residents over several generations. This will provide a fairly accurate portrayal of the culture. This will add to the understanding of small-town history and preservation as a whole because it appears that this is a topic not often discussed. The cultures of small-town America have not appeared to be a popular academic discussion. I hope that this thesis will dissolve some of the stereotypes surrounding small towns and prove that they can have their own unique cultures that added to the nation's history. It is important to note that I am an insider due to my close ties to both the town and the family I am putting forth to represent it. Being a part of this family and the community may cause me to see the town from a different perspective than an outsider might. I aim to be unbiased while evaluating the information I have collected, but it is important to recognize that it is difficult to remain completely impartial when writing about a personal topic such as this.

It is possible that there are sources pertaining to this topic that I have not yet discovered. There may be other writing on the history of small towns that I have not come across in my research because I have not yet found the right place to look. There may also be other examples of programs or small towns that have done well in preserving small towns. However, as I have not found many sources of this yet, I will continue to explore the argument that small towns have not been explored or preserved historically as well as they could be.

**David Leroy Eidson**

David "Leroy" Eidson, one of my paternal great-grandfathers, was born October 7, 1922, in Saluda, South Carolina. He came from a family of farmers and grew up during the Great Depression. Leroy grew up working on farms, both those belonging to his family and those of his friends near where he lived. He would often pick cotton and tend to vegetable gardens. They obtained their food from their own gardens and would preserve them in jars, because they were not wealthy enough to own their own refrigerator. Leroy moved to Graniteville from Batesburg, in Saluda County, in order to work for the Graniteville Company.[16] His grandfather, West Eidson, had lived in Saluda, so the family had resided in that area for at least three generations by the time he moved. He was a year younger than I am at the writing of this work, when he moved away from all his family in search of new employment.[17]

Leroy began working for the Graniteville Company in 1941 as a laborer in the Gregg division preparation department. He had moved from picking cotton, to working in a mill where the cotton was used to produce clothing. The primary purpose of this department was to ensure that all dye was distributed to the cloth, mostly denim, properly and evenly.[18] He worked a machine that would check for imperfections in the cloth. This division was also responsible for preparing the cloth to be dyed. Experts have broken the preparatory process into two broad categories, the cleaning processes and the whitening processes. The cleaning processes focused on removing impurities, both manually and with chemicals. The cleaning processes focus on removing color from the material in order to prepare it to be recolored to the pigment the company desires. This can be done by removing color matter or chemically improving the whiteness of a material.[19] Based on great-aunt Zell's stories, it is more likely that Leroy worked with chemicals. There were not as many safety precautions at the time, so the workers did not use any safety gear, despite the use of strong chemicals.[20]

Once in Graniteville, Leroy met his wife and had two daughters, one of whom is my paternal grandmother. She and her sister, Zell, would often take Leroy his lunch when they were out of school. My aunt remembers handing him his lunch over the fence, since he was not permitted to leave the premises during the workday. By the time he retired in 1985, he had risen to the position of supervisor within the same department.[21] Leroy's retirement may have been encouraged by a change in ownership, which occurred in the same year. Since his retirement, ownership changed several times. The building in which he spent 44 years of his life working is still standing, but unfortunately, has been allowed to deteriorate. There were multiple mills owned by the Graniteville Company in the area, but my great-aunt Zell lamented that his building was "the most beautiful manufacturing building here."[22]

In 2017, an article was published by a local news station that discussed possible preservation ideas for the town. It explained that the Horse Creek Trust wanted to re-purpose the various mills previously owned by the Graniteville Company. It speaks briefly on their belief that the Graniteville Mill would be a good candidate for loft apartments, with "tables and the umbrellas and the shops" outside in the plaza. While this idea represents what I believe many locals dream for the Graniteville Mill, the article does not give any information concerning these dreams being put into action. [23] Additionally, *Preservation Magazine* published an article in 2019 on Graniteville and the possible restoration projects that some were hoping for. The article quotes a couple of locals, who expressed their desires for a rehabilitation project to kick start the town back into the busy and bustling community they remember living in prior to the train accident. However, the article does not include any plans that the owners have created to restore Graniteville's mill.[24] While these articles provide hope that one day the mill may be repurposed, as it appears others are also hoping for this outcome, they are a couple of years old, and I have yet to come across any sources that indicate this will be taking place in the near future.

Leroy remained in Graniteville until his death in 2020. He moved away from his family to Graniteville early in his life for the chance to find a life outside of farming. He built a life in Graniteville that he shared with multiple generations. He had a long career with the Graniteville Company and found his wife there. He raised two daughters, enjoyed watching three grandsons grow up, and had seven great grandchildren (including the author) that he got to know and have relationships with. The roots that this side of the family has with Graniteville started with him, and my love for the town is also partly rooted in my love for him. All of this started with a job with the Graniteville Company. It would be nice to see the large historic building where he worked be put to new use for the community but driving past the building every time, I return home is a nice reminder and connection to a great-grandfather that I knew and loved.

**Daniel Carpenter**

Daniel Carpenter, another one of my paternal great-grandfathers, was born January 2, 1918, in rural Aiken County. He attended the Graniteville public school through the fourth grade, at which time he left school to help the family with farming. Growing up during the Great Depression, Daniel and his family raised cows, pigs, chickens, and vegetables for their food. They also sold some of what they produced in order to procure income. This farming lifestyle did not leave them any extra spending money but allowed the family to be well fed and taken care of during a period when many Americans struggled. In 1938, Daniel volunteered with the army at twenty years old. He left the service after two years but was drafted back after the attack on Pearl Harbor. His job during the war was to drive transportation trucks in Europe.[25]

After he was discharged from the army at the end of World War II, Daniel began working in the maintenance department at the Graniteville Company. My grandfather does not remember a specific date but estimates that Daniel began his work with the company in 1945. He started as a laborer and retired around 1990 as a supervisor. He was originally working in the carpentry shop but later transferred to work with sheet metal. It was in the sheet metal shop where he was promoted to a foreman and remained until his retirement.[26] The maintenance department was responsible for ensuring all of the mills within the Graniteville Company were running properly, so he performed jobs at all of them during his 45 years with the department. However, he worked primarily out of the maintenance building. Unfortunately, this structure has been torn down, but some of the other mills he worked on are still there today.[27]

After his retirement, Daniel bought a pond site in Graniteville where he built a cabin, raised cows, and kept a garden. This was a hobby that reminds me of his youth when he would perform many of the same tasks with his family on their farm. He passed away in 2002 at the age of 84. He left the pond property to his four grandchildren David Seymour (my father), Kevin Seymour, Michael Seymour, and Linda Daniels. However, they did not have much time to spend at the pond, and eventually only my Uncle Kevin utilized the land consistently. This led to their decision to sell the land. I am grateful that I had the opportunity to visit the pond while I was old enough to remember it. It was interesting to get to see where my great-grandfather enjoyed so much of his time in retirement. While our family no longer owns the pond my great-grandfather enjoyed, there are examples in the family where the activities enjoyed there are still being performed today. My father and uncle both enjoy fishing and have taught the skill to their children. Additionally, my father and my great-aunt Zell enjoy gardening.[28]

**Education**

Another tie I have to this town is that my paternal grandfather, Jim Seymour, attended the local school here. There is a long history of the importance of education being stressed in Graniteville, even from the town's beginning. While deeming school important is not a unique idea, I believe my grandfather's enthusiasm for education may have roots in the standards set by the town. William Gregg, the founder of Graniteville, also built a school for the town. Graniteville Academy educated the children of Graniteville until it closed in 1922, after which the building served as a community center. In 1982, a newspaper article explained that the building was being used as a club for senior citizens. Some of the children who attended the school there were able to then use the building later in life as a social club.[29] Therefore, the positive impact Gregg imparted on the children within the community continued throughout their lives, even years after the school had halted classes. Gregg was very involved with the education of children within Graniteville and even tried to provide educational opportunities to children living in the nearby country. During his daily visits to the mill, he would stop by the school at recess time. He enjoyed playing with the children, and often brought them a large tub of peaches from his own garden. He would even go into the classroom for discussions with the students.[30]

Miss Jo's Candy Store is another piece of local history that was tied to education and unique to the community as a whole. Most of the children remember the store for its candy, but the primary purpose of the store was to provide schoolbooks for the children at the Old Graniteville Academy and other schools nearby. George Washington Ernest Thorpe and Martha Steele were a couple from Graniteville who married and moved to the nearby city of Aiken. There they opened a general store that sold seed to farmers, groceries for the majority of the community, and schoolbooks. They were pushed to open a store in Graniteville by their relatives. After they agreed and the store first opened, it was run by Miss Josephine Thorpe. I presume this was the inspiration for the store's name. Many of the old books that were used in the Graniteville Academy had the stamp "J. Thorpe Book-Seller and Stationer. School Books A Specialty. Graniteville, S.C." While this store may have been central to the education system in Graniteville and the surrounding area, most of the fond memories of this establishment revolve around the candy store. The building was removed to Warrenville in 1952, and unfortunately later razed in 2002.[31] The Thorpe's willingness to open a new store to fill a need for the children of Graniteville portray the way this community was tight-knit, cared for each other, and prioritized the education of their children.

Gregg took the education of children very seriously, requiring all children in the town to attend school regularly. This may have been one of the first compulsory education systems in the South.[32] His employees were fined five cents for each day that their child missed school. There are stories of Gregg finding children who were attempting to skip school at the "ole swimming hole" and personally brought them back to the school office for a "licking." There was one boy who often snuck away from the school to go fishing. When Gregg heard about this, he decided to catch the boy in the act. "Gregg lay in wait for him on the road and as the boy came from the bushes beside the stream, seized him, lifted him into the buggy and drove to the mill office."[33] Because the usual punishments for this child had not been effective in keeping him in school, Gregg had him stand on a bookkeeper's desk for a new form of punishment. The employees were instructed to ask the boy questions as they passed by the desk. Each time Gregg would explain "There stands a boy that would rather go fishing than get an education." After a time, the boy asked to be let down, promising that his days of skipping school were over.[34] The importance of education was embedded in the founding of Graniteville, with Gregg stressing and enforcing this principle. This strong emphasis on education is one that is shared by my grandfather, Jim Seymour.

Jim graduated high school from Leavelle McCampbell in 1963 and became the first generation in his family to attend college. His father, Daniel Carpenter, attended school through the fourth grade. His father-in-law, Leroy Eidson, attended school through the ninth grade. Jim earned his B.S. in Electrical Engineering from the University of South Carolina in 1967 and earned his professional engineering license in 1973. This required that he worked for five years, then took the National Engineer Society Test. He spent an entire day taking the examination but passed it on his first attempt.[35] Jim has always been a big advocate for higher education for his children and grandchildren. He always tried to teach me to value education. I remember when he encouraged me to go to college and find a career that I could enjoy while supporting myself. His encouragement has not been in vain. Both of his sons earned college degrees, five of his grandchildren are currently attending college (myself included), and his last grandchild is preparing to follow the tradition.

**Community Togetherness**

Togetherness is another theme in my family. Growing up, my extended family lived close together and saw each other often. Until I was eighteen, we would sit at least once a year (usually at Christmas) with five generations at the dinner table, four who have lived in Graniteville, and the other visiting from out of town. I grew up going to school with many of my cousins and lived within a ten-minute drive to the homes of most family members. My grandparents lived only a couple houses down the street. There has always been an emphasis on togetherness, even with the few family members who do not live in the area. I have met many people who have not been so fortunate and whose families are not close, so I am thankful for my close family relationships. However, being part of a tight-knit community that takes care of each other is not a trait reserved only for biological family. In a way, Graniteville has been a lot like a family because the people care for one another.

An example of Graniteville's family-like character is portrayed through the story of "The Little

Boy." In the oldest section of the Graniteville cemetery, there is a gravestone that simply reads "The Little Boy - 1855." The child had been traveling alone via train when he became ill. He was taken off of the train at Graniteville by the local women, who then tried to nurse him back to health. The poor boy was too sick to tell the women his name, where he was traveling to, or the names of any relatives. He died without the townspeople knowing who he was, or where to find his family. The women who had cared for him collected silk and satin scraps that they used to line a coffin the men built for him. The people of Graniteville then came together to buy him the tombstone that still stands today. Flowers continue to be placed on the boy's grave by locals who know the story of "The Little Boy."[36] The people of Graniteville were kind, caring for a sick child that they unofficially adopted into their community.

Graniteville is still a tight-knit community because it has always put an emphasis on staying connected. Years ago, the Graniteville Company released a *Graniteville Bulletin* to keep the community up to date on various company and local news. Local poems, the student honor roll, and lists of servicemen from the community are among the many pieces of news reported in this bulletin. During my research, I found an issue from the 1940s, which is around the time both of my great-grandfathers began working with the company. This included a 1942 article from the Gregg Dyeing Division which discussed the women who had begun working within the division. The article included a photograph of them, and it explained their willingness to work in order to fill the positions left by men who had gone to fight in World War II. During World War II, the bulletin would print letters that local men sent home while they were away fighting. These letters helped keep the community updated on how the young men were faring. Several men thanked the community in their letters for Christmas cards and their own copies of the *Graniteville Bulletin* that the community sent them. This shows how even in times of war, the Graniteville community remained tight-knit and cared for each other. Despite being far away, the men who served were cared for and remained an integral part of the community.[37]

There was also an article titled "Old Records." This article explained that the company had realized that being the oldest cotton manufacturer in the South, they played an important role in the history of the Southern textile industry. They began collecting old company records and requested that anyone willing to share their old family records pertaining to the company, to help. The president, S.H. Swint, stated that "someday we hope to have a building which will serve as a permanent home for these relics. Until that time they will be carefully preserved in the main office."[38] It was fulfilling to read this at the Aiken County Historical Museum, a local museum that had dedicated a small room to doing just that. While this may not be a whole building dedicated to the preservation of Graniteville's history, it is a start to what Swint had hoped for.

There are other examples that portray how Graniteville has continued to be a close community in recent years. One of these examples includes a local restaurant that has been a part of the community since 1946, called the Blue Top. They celebrated their 75$^{th}$ anniversary of their opening in 2021. This small restaurant is known for their burgers, fries, and other fried foods. I grew up eating there and have many fond memories of family dinners at the establishment. Every time I go, my grandparents know almost every customer inside. It was a popular place to spend time when they were in high school. The students often went there after football games and would even sneak away from school to have a burger or hotdog for lunch. The previous owner, Ms. Linda, is an old friend of my grandparents.

She has now passed down the business to Mrs. Renee, the third generation in the family, who my father went to school with. My father also runs into familiar faces at the Blue Top. The fourth generation, whom I attended school with, has started to participate in the family business and may one day continue the family tradition. The Blue Top is a popular restaurant for Graniteville's inhabitants, and it has a long history of being a meeting place, bringing the town together.

Another example of Graniteville remaining a close community in more recent years is that of Ms. Jewel. She enjoyed baking and was famous for her delicious homemade cakes. Anytime there was an event, members of the town went to her house and requested a cake. They would choose from whatever options she had available in her freezer at the time and pay her for it. My grandparents remember this fondly, and my dad still laments that he never got the recipe for her coconut cake. Everyone in town knew Ms. Jewel and turned to her for their celebration events.

**Utopia Movement**

Graniteville was not immune to the problems that can arise in small towns. One such problem is the bubble-like nature of its social environment. Being a small-town with a tight-knit community can sometimes create a metaphorical bubble because there is such a unique culture and community within the town. This bubble may have created an insular community, where people focus on their own heritage and struggle to see the significance of other places. This bubble mentality also means that the people of Graniteville do not try to relate the significance of their town to the outside world and consequently, outsiders do not understand the culture within Graniteville and therefore cannot be expected to understand why it is special.

Gregg helped to create this bubble and determine what the culture of the small town would be like. He built a school, churches, the mill, and housing that were all constructed in the same Gothic Revival architectural style for the people to live in. This prevented employees from seeking places outside of Graniteville. He required education to be a priority for the children and prohibited the drinking of alcohol.[39] He also provided space for a community garden within Graniteville, so the community could tend it and enjoy the fruits and vegetables that were grown there.[40] Gregg interviewed each person that wanted to work for his company. He believed that maintaining a certain moral character within the town was necessary to create a model community.[41] What resulted was a small mill town where almost everyone either worked or had a family member who worked in the mill. They attended the same churches, their children attended the same schools, they all shopped at the same store, and gardened together. Graniteville has continued to maintain this level of civic closeness and cohesion, even in recent years. The legacy of the Blue Top and Ms. Jewel's cakes are a testament to this. The close-knit feel of Graniteville has remained strong.

Gregg was not alone in trying to create a utopia at this time. There was a movement in the nineteenth century to create utopian communities in response to the Industrial Revolution. Industrialization led to pollution of air and water, which many workers lived in constantly due to their homes being in close proximity to the factories in which they worked. Sewage could be found leaking into various water supplies, while human and animal waste could be found coating alleyways. Conditions in the city proved to be so unhealthy that it drove out the wealthy, who had the means to reside outside of the city and commute.[42] In his work *Victorian Visions of Suburban Utopia*, Nathaniel Walker explains Robert Owen's argument that with the increased use of machinery during the Industrial Revolution, human labor decreased in value, which resulted in poverty and poor living and working conditions for many wage workers. Walker also explains that the quick influx of workers to the city in order to reside close to their factory jobs further added to the unsanitary conditions of the city.[43] When one looks at the horrific living conditions that were created in response to the Industrial Revolution, it is easy to understand how some may have looked back longingly at a time before cities were polluted by modernity. It is possible that Gregg was inspired by others within this movement, and therefore Graniteville is another result of the ideas brought forth by it.

Robert Owen is an example of an Englishman attempting to create a utopia at this time. In 1841, he published *A Development of the Principles and Plans on which to Establish Self-supporting Home Colonies,* where he described what he believed would be an ideal society.[44] Owen attempted to instill his odd ideals for a utopian community not only in the mill town of New Lanark, located in Scotland, but also in New Harmony, Indiana.[45] His distaste for industrial cities is what led him to create these experiments, yet he was not anti-industrialization, as is seen in both of his mill town experiments.[46] His purchase of and relocation to New Harmony brought him and his ideals to America in 1825, resulting in his notoriety reaching a larger scale that reached past his home country.[47] This leaves several years for Owen's notorious ideals to be discovered by Gregg before his founding of Graniteville in 1845.[48]

In his preface, Owen lists twelve adjustments to society that are necessary to create this ideal society, which he refers to as the millennium. The first listed is that there should be no slavery or inequality in condition, with age and experience being exceptions to this rule.[49] This is interesting considering his seventh call of action, which is to abandon one part of society paying money wages to another part of society. Owen argued that this practice "led to far greater injustice, oppression, degradation, crime, and misery, than existed, at any former period; even when slavery was the *general* practice of the human race."[50] His comparison of society after industrialization to being worse than a society that uses slavery, after he condemns the practice of slavery or similar forms of inequality, is telling of how horrible he believed society had become.

Gregg also chose to free labor; however, I believe his intentions were different than Owen's. He wanted to create an ideal town for poor whites, so they would have more opportunities in life. However, there was a black population within the town. While I am uncertain when this diversity came to Graniteville, there is record of a Black community residing in Graniteville. Records claim that this community was named "Boogie-Boo" after one of its settlers.[51] Both men promoted not using enslaved labor, but Owen spoke from an abolitionists point of view while Gregg spoke more as an advocate for poor whites. They had similar ideas for different purposes, and Owen would not have approved of Gregg's approach. Gregg did not rely on enslaved labor to run his mill, but instead he paid wages to his workers. This is a practice that Owen strongly disapproved of.

Gregg paid his employees in a unique way. For a time, Graniteville Company employees were paid with Graniteville coins, which were called "Boogaloos" by the locals. Each mill under the Graniteville Company had their own Boogaloo coins, each portraying the first letter of the mills name (G for Graniteville, L for Langley, etc.). These coins were taken at the company store in town and were not transferable.[52] This means that the employees were unable to exchange the coins for traditional currency, and therefore were unable to use those wages outside of stores provided by the Graniteville Company.[53] I struggled to find specific dates concerning when these coins were used because the local archives and the coins did not provide any dates. However, my grandfather, Jim, and my great-aunt Zell both were unaware that these coins existed, so Boogaloos were likely used as currency at the founding of the town and were retired before my great-grandfathers came to Graniteville in the 1940s (Figure 3.2).[54] A newspaper article from 1935 discusses an issue at the time concerning the coins. In 1935, a judge determined that the local stores were not required to trade the boogaloo coins for traditional cash. This indicates that the coins were in use at the time and did prevent employees from taking their business elsewhere.[55] However, the use of their own currency further encouraged the bubble within which the Graniteville community grew.

Figure 3.2: Boogaloo Coins. Photograph by the author.

Owen's second call to action was to provide improved education to the mass of the people. He argued that while many people have agreed that education is important, "there is not one educational establishment known, that is calculated to train individuals, from birth, to become rational men and women."[56] Gregg also made Graniteville's education system better than the standard at that time. His implementation of the first effective compulsory education system in the South portrays his agreement that education should be improved. However, while Gregg's desire was to provide access to a higher quality education would improve the opportunities children would have in the future, Owen had a different reason for wanting to improve education. He believed that it was necessary to understand the science of human nature so that society could produce the "superior character" within each person.[57] While their reasons differed, both Gregg and Owen agreed that education and strict morals were necessary for creating utopian communities.

Owen's ninth call to action was "to form the external arrangements around every-one, from birth, to insure to him the best *physical, moral, intellectual, and practical education,* that his constitution, or natural faculties, when born, will admit." Owen believed that the character of people could be formed throughout their lives by society. That a person can be influenced by their environment.[58] It is likely that Gregg also adopted this idea for Graniteville. The media expressed their delight in the beautiful structures Gregg built for the town, including the mill houses he provided for his workers in the Gothic Revival style. My great-aunt Zell describes the Graniteville Mill as being one of the most beautiful mills constructed in the area.[59] One newspaper article in particular refers to Graniteville as a "storybook town" with "storybook houses."[60] Gregg's decision to construct mill houses in a Gothic Revival style was likely intentional and influenced by the Utopia Movement.

Many advocates of Gothic Revival architecture who were also anti-industrialist and anti-capitalist. This movement aimed to recreate the societal standards of the Middle Ages and repent from the undesirable lifestyle of the nineteenth century that was brewed by industrialization.[61] Owen attempted to put his ideals to practice in New Lanark, Scotland. He inherited the New Lanark Company in 1799 from his father-in-law. Owen was a paternalistic entrepreneur early in his career who believed that the wealthy had a responsibility to provide for dependents by "balancing benevolence and authority."[62] In return, the lower classed dependents owed their loyalty and obedience to their wealthy caretaker. This patriarchal system is similar to feudal hierarchal systems.[63] New Lanark is similar to Graniteville in the ways that Gregg and Owen attempted to create patriarchal utopias.

In New Lanark, Owen valued educating children. He acknowledged the difficulty children had in balancing school and work and suggested that children ages 10 to 12 only work in the mills part time. Unfortunately, this policy was never enacted, most likely due to Owen's partners expressing distaste for the idea. However, the children of New Lanark received an average of eight years of education. This was significant because in the United Kingdom most urban working-class children only received schooling on Sundays, while childhood education in rural settings depended on harvest schedules.[64] Owen's dedication to educating was a trait that Gregg shared and put into action in Graniteville.

In addition to the social ideas that New Lanark and Graniteville had in common, they were also similar in their physical construction. Owen insisted on supporting education and a "community feeling" despite his partners' reluctance to do so.[65] Owen commissioned a building in 1809 to be "an extensive Store Cellar, a Public Kitchen, Eating and Exercise Room, a School, Lecture Room and Church."[66] Gregg similarly provided structures like this for Graniteville. It is highly likely that his idea to construct a school, church, public garden for fresh food, and a company store came from Owen's example in New Lanark. A second example of an Englishman trying to create a utopian community during this period was A. Welby Pugin. He believed that industrialization had corrupted cities, and that refuge could only be found by turning to the past.[67] Pugin is a striking contrast to Owen, because he was not against cities themselves, only anti-industrialization. In his book, *Contrasts*, published in 1841, Pugin talks about church architecture of the Middle Ages, which is Gothic. He attributes most of the loss of this architecture to Protestantism and Paganism. He claims that "everything glorious about the English churches is Catholic, everything debased and hideous, Protestant."[68]

Throughout *Contrasts,* Pugin attributes the loss of Gothic architecture to what he believes is the perversion of the Christian faith.[69] If this movement believed the end of society's purity at the time can be visually marked by the loss of Gothic architecture, then they must associate Gothic architecture with social and religious purity. Could this have led Pugin, Owens, and Gregg to believe that Gothic architecture had purifying qualities itself, if they are artistic creations of a pure faith? The architecture was tarnished when the religion and modern morality became skewed. Therefore, according to their rational, using Gothic architecture would be a step toward fixing religion, and by extension, society.

Pugin, along with other advocates of the Gothic Revival style at this time, disapproved of society relying on modern industrialism and capitalism. Wiener argues that "as an antidote to the present they [architects] recreated the past as an ideal world of preindustrial simplicity."[70] Weiner argues that the Gothic Revival was part of a larger movement that was reacting to the Industrial Revolution.[71] This is an example of how these men believed Gothic architecture could better society, even from the downfalls of the Industrial Revolution. Pugin's abhorrence of architecture outside of the Gothic style is apparent in his analysis of the Crystal Palace, constructed for the Great Exhibition of 1851. He describes the palace as a "glass monster" and considers it a product of a soulless age.[72]

Pugin may have also inspired Gregg while he was founding Graniteville. Both Pugin and Owen published the texts I referenced in 1841. Gregg began building his mill and the town in 1845, after the Graniteville Manufacturing Company Charter was granted.[73] Since Graniteville came only a few years after these publications, it is probable that the similarities between Graniteville and the utopian idea from this movement means he was influenced by them. While he did not copy their ideals exactly, it seems he adopted what aspects of their utopian ideas he agreed with and left behind those he did not. The housing he built for the inhabitants of Graniteville were built in the Gothic Revival style. The original houses, constructed in 1847, were located on Gregg Street and called "Blue Row" due to the blue wash used on all the dwellings.[74] More mill houses were constructed in 1907, one of which became my great-grandfather Leroy's home for 54 years. He moved into the home from another mill house across the street in 1966, and it remained in his possession until his death in 2020. [75]Gregg's decision to use Gothic Revival architecture is significant considering that others at the time were also using the Gothic Revival style in attempts to create a utopian community.

My family is an example of what Gregg was trying to accomplish. My great-grandfathers left the Great Depression and World War II when they came to

Graniteville. They transitioned from farmers to employees of a large manufacturing company and became part of a tight-knit community. Their children then had the opportunity to attend school longer than either of them had the chance to. My grandfather was the first on that side of the family to attend college, and he eventually became an engineer. The generations that followed have enjoyed the opportunities to attend college and study for a career of their choosing. My great-grandfathers started off their lives as poor farmers during the Great Depression but worked hard and found new opportunities for themselves and the generations that followed in Graniteville. Because the trend of building utopian communities was a response to the problems of the Industrial Revolution, it is peculiar that Gregg desired to bring industrialization to the South while also trying to create his own utopia *through* industrializing the South. However, the use of Gothic Revival architecture and the principles he enforced within Graniteville are related to those of Owen and Pugin.

**Significance**

Why does all this matter? How is Graniteville and my family's story, which is connected to the town, significant? One determinant of significance that Graniteville meets is novelty. The founding of the town itself is rooted in novelty. When Gregg brought manufacturing to the South, it was a rare occurrence that many Southerners did not approve of. As Gregg went on to build the town around the mill, novelty was still apparent. The mandatary school system he enforced at the school he built was one of the first successful systems in the South. Another determinant of significance Graniteville meets is effect. My family is an example of how the town affected people who lived there. Gregg built the town with the hopes of improving South Carolina's economy and improving the lives of poorer whites living in the South. Both of my great-grandfathers left a life of farming to work at the Graniteville Mill. By raising their families there, they instilled education as an institution of great importance, which originated with Gregg. This resulted in my grandfather Jim becoming the first person on the paternal side of my family to go to college. Since then, both of his sons followed in his footsteps and all of his grandchildren are working to earn their own degrees.

A third determinant of significance for Graniteville is applicability. The culture that made up the Graniteville community at its founding, when my great-grandfathers moved to the town, and the present all have similar characteristics. Education and community togetherness are two big themes that have survived the test of time and continue to have a place in Graniteville, and I plan to continue the tradition of instilling these characteristics into the future generations. Graniteville is historically significant in multiple ways. Its novelty, effect, and applicability solidify this argument. If this small town can have such a large role in history, it is likely that other small towns also have important contributions to history that are waiting to be explored. I believe this imparts a responsibility for us to discover these contributions. Including the history of small towns in our history as a whole will provide a more diverse and well-rounded understanding of the past.

**Conclusion**

Graniteville as a case study proves that a small-town has a lot of history that is significant and relevant to the history of America as a whole. It was one of the first manufacturing companies that brought industry to the South, and at a time when many were actively against the idea.[76] Additionally, Graniteville introduced new ways to improve education. The town's school was one of the first in the South to have a compulsory education system.[77] Thirdly, the town was influenced by the Utopia Movement that emerged after the Industrial Revolution. These three examples portray how Graniteville has influenced life in the American South through economics, education, and a social movement from the 1840s.

Graniteville has attempted to preserve its cultural heritage; however, I believe that more can be done to aid in this endeavor. The Graniteville Mill and some of the original mill houses that were constructed for its workers were added to the National Register of Historic Places.[78] Some of the locals have put together books made up of old photographs along with a basic overview of the history of the town.[79] One of these books was written by Sue McLaughlin and Sharon McLaughlin and is titled *Reflections of Graniteville.* Within this book the women collected photographs, legends, and history from a multitude of Graniteville citizens.[80] The second book by Jean Clark Boyd, is *A Pictorial Timeline of Graniteville, South Carolina 1845-1996.* It was published by the Horse Creek Historical Society.[81] Thirdly, the Aiken County Historical Museum has dedicated a room to Graniteville, as it is included in Aiken County. While the room may be small, it is still an important achievement for such a small town, especially when one considers that the town of Aiken itself has such a long and rich history that the museum is dedicated to. The museum even has a vertical file on Graniteville in their archive. All of these efforts have been impressive strides in preservation for a small town.

Despite the preservation efforts that have been made, I believe that more can be done to better preserve Graniteville and its heritage. The original mill that sits in the center of town is empty and has been left unoccupied for years. A lack of use and care can cause the mill to deteriorate and no longer be cared for by community. My great-aunt Zell has stated that the mill has become "an eyesore" for the town. While there have been a few articles discussing the possibility of turning the mill into apartments, it has yet to occur and seems unlikely in the future. I have reached out to the planning director of Aiken County, and while he sounded optimistic that another mill in the area may be repurposed into apartments through adaptive reuse, he has not yet heard anything to indicate that this will take place with the Graniteville Mill.[82] While it seems unlikely that the mill will be repurposed for apartments, I would love to see it brought to life again through some form of reuse. This would allow the building to have a contemporary relevance and increase the community's appreciation of it. Many buildings that were part of the Graniteville Company have been razed, including the maintenance building where my great-grandfather, Daniel Carpenter, worked.[83] This loss of architecture makes the original mill structure even more valued, as it is one of the remaining manufacturing structures.

Furthermore, I believe that a better job could be done educating the local community about its history. Despite having lived in Graniteville for several years and having family members live there throughout my entire life, I was unaware of the majority of Graniteville's past. I have deep roots in the town, four generations, and I only knew the stories told to me by my grandparents and great-aunt. I think that in addition to hearing family stories, more can be done to educate my generation and younger about the history of Graniteville and its culture. The local schools could spend time on this history, even if it is only for a day trip to the Aiken County Historical Museum. Students typically study South Carolina history at some point in their public education within the state, so involving the museum in this process would give students exposure to Graniteville history. Introducing students to local traditions, such as visiting the Blue Top, would immerse them in the community and help support local businesses that have been a part of Graniteville for generations.

There are several ways I plan on preserving and passing down my culture to my future children and grandchildren. Explaining to the next generation why this town has been so important to my family is the first step. Secondly, I will instill in the next generation an importance of family and remaining close to each other. I will continue the tradition of big family dinners and having extended family play a role in their lives. I plan on sharing with children the joys of visits to the Blue Top, tasting Mrs. Jewel's cake recipes that my grandmother passed down to me, and taking them to the Graniteville Room in the Aiken County Historical Museum. I plan to continue stressing the importance of education. From Gregg to my grandfather Jim, to my father and uncle, and myself, valuing education and the opportunities it can provide has been a prime focus for the Graniteville community. I hope that the education for future generations of my family will include the history of Graniteville. Understanding how and why the town came to be allows for a deeper appreciation of the impacts it had on my family.

Graniteville is an example of a small town with a rich history that contributes to the history of America. The discoveries of how the town contributes to the economy, education system, and a social movement help to shed light on each subject. There are many other small towns in the South that have their own histories, each deserving of preservation and could also aid in better understanding other historical topics. Understanding American history requires that we study each part that makes up the whole, and this includes small towns.

## Chapter 4: The Klocks: Pioneers of the Mohawk Valley

By Gabriella Rowsam

Many people think that their family's history has little impact on their lives in the present. However, I have always believed that one cannot truly understand who they are before they understand who their ancestors were. Some people can't learn about their biological ancestors, and I don't think that by any means that one's ancestors define who they are, but those who are fortunate enough to have knowledge about their lineage should take the time to learn about their origins. I was 11 years old when I started asking family members why everyone always pronounced our surname wrong and why it wasn't spelled the way it sounded. This led to my paternal grandfather giving me a long rectangular scrapbook that was held together with green shoelaces that read *Rowsam Genealogy'* across the front. Up until this moment, no one in my family had ever discussed the origins of our heritage with me. It was filled with the names of my ancestors from upstate New York. It was mind boggling to me that this book held the names of people from whom I was related. I spent hours looking over the pages, learning names, and analyzing the numerous historic photographs of my ancestors that my grandparents passed down to me.

I can recall coming across my four times great-grandmother's name, Magdalena Elizabeth Klock, and wondering how peculiar it was. On her side of the family tree, she was the last of the line. Something about her maiden name intrigued me and I decided to do research on where the Klock name came from. Through my research, I was able to go back five more generations to the Klocks who first settled in North America. How could this lineage have been forgotten? The Klocks were

German Palatines who fled their homeland in the early eighteenth century due to the warfare that plagued the country. Through literature, historic documents, and a fortified homestead, this chapter will delve into the Klock family lineage; investigating how they came to settle in the Mohawk River Valley in New York, their involvement in the French & Indian War and American Revolution. The history of this family is largely intertwined with the history of the British North American colonies and the United States. By better understanding their story one can better understand the history of this country.

**Prior Academic Research**[1]

The history of German Palatines that settled in the British North American Colonies during the early part of the eighteenth century is a topic that has been effectively researched in the past by multiple scholars. These sources help paint a picture of what life was like for the German Palatines that came to settle and start a new life in a foreign land. A good amount of research has been done on this topic because these German Palatines left their impact on what later became the United States. The Klocks, my ancestors, were German Palatines who settled in New York along the Mohawk River Valley. A great deal of research has been done on this family, specifically due to their connection with the fortified homestead, Fort Klock (Figure 4.1), that lies along the Mohawk River, but a competent story of what their lives were like during the eighteenth century has yet to be told. The secondary sources listed below will be used to help better understand what life was like for a German Palatine pioneer that left their homelands due to treacherous wars and who fled to the colonies to escape it only to again be faced with the tragedies of the French & Indian War as and American Revolution.

Figure 4.1: Fort Klock, U.S. Route 5, St. Johnsville, Montgomery County, New York. Historic American Buildings Survey, 1940. Library of Congress Prints and Photographs Division.

When it comes to the eighteenth century historic fabric of the German Palatines that settled along the Mohawk River Valley not much of it remains. The majority of it was constructed of wood and destroyed by the wars that ravaged the landscape. One aspect that survived is Fort Klock. It is a rare example of a fortified homestead that was used by the German Palatines to protect themselves, their families, and their neighbors from the treacherous frontier that laid beyond its walls. Fort Klock is one of two fortified homesteads from the mid eighteen century in New York State that are on the National Register of Historic Places.

One of the sources used for Fort Klock's National Register Nomination was the book *Forts and Firesides of the Mohawk Country, New York: Stories and Pictures of Landmarks of the Pre-Revolutionary War Period Throughout the Mohawk Valley and Surrounding Countryside, Including Some Historical and Genealogical Mention During the Post-War Period,* by John J. Vrooman. He writes about the Revolutionary

War and the historic landmarks that are connected to it. Fort Klock is described in this book in great detail and Vrooman also makes note of the famous American figures who sought shelter behind its walls.

*The History of the Mohawk Valley: Gateway to the West, 1614-1925*, covering the six counties of Schenectady, Schoharie, Montgomery, Fulton, Herkimer and Oneida is a book written by Nelson Green. In it he discusses the rich history of the counties that make up the Mohawk River Valley. This source discusses the German Palatines were settlers in upstate New York, which was considered a gateway to the west. How the Palatines were involved in the French & Indian War and American Revolution is also covered.

There is also *The Early Eighteenth Century Palatine Emigration: A British Government Redemptioner Project To Manufacture Naval Stores,* by Walter Allen Knittle. The author first examines the cause of the Palatine immigration and how they sought refuge in The Netherlands and England. Knittle covers how the British transported the German Palatines to their colonies to produce naval stores. It discusses the indentured servitude they experienced when they reached the British colonies. This source offers a great deal of insight into what life was like living in the East and West Camps along the Hudson River. The later Palatine settlements on the frontier are also discussed.

In 1972, the State of New York's Parks and Recreation department published *The Mohawk Valley and the American Revolution.* This publication describes how the settlers of the Mohawk Valley played a part in the American Revolution and the founding of the United States of America. It also looks back to how the River Valley was settled by European colonists. The types of housing which the settlers of this region are also discussed at great length. Hank Jones even references Knittle's work in his own book, *The Palatine Families of*

*New York: A Study of the German Immigrants Who Arrived in Colonial New York 1710*. This is one of the more recent works done on this topic as it was done in 1985. Jones went into great depth researching hundreds of German Palatine families who made the journey across the Atlantic during this period, going as far as to figuring out which German villages they hailed from. He speaks of the propaganda that persuaded the German Palatines to risk their lives and travel thousands of miles across the Atlantic to be able to start a new life in the "paradise" that was the British colonies. His work is very thorough, but there are errors that can be found that would have been hard to work through with the resources available to scholars at the time this was published.

*A Time of Terror: The Story of Colonel Jacob Klock's Regiment and The People They Protected* is self-published by A. J. Berry. While this book wasn't written that long ago there have been great strides made in historical research since then that may have changed some of its content. For example, the author believes that Colonel Jacob Klock may have been born around the 1740s, but sources on Ancestery.com say he was born in 1701. This may be due to the fact that this family regularly reused names throughout its generations. This piece offers a great deal of information about what life was like living in the Mohawk River Valley during the mid to late eighteenth century. Berry not only discusses the militia and their stories of the battles, but also what life was like for women during the Revolution. It discusses the fortified homesteads in the area, the majority of which are no longer standing. Many of the people who settled in St. Johnsville were German Palatines and Berry discusses the types of farm buildings they used to harvest and store grain. The author also points out that some people living in the area were Loyalists who supported the British during the American

Revolution. This book offers a wealth of knowledge that is very valuable to this paper.

*George Klock, the Canajoharie Mohawks, and the Good Ship Sir William Johnson: Land, Legitimacy, and Community in the Eighteenth-Century Mohawk Valley* is an article by David L. Preston in the *New York History Journal.* This essay describes the journey of the Klocks to the Mohawk Valley and their interactions with Native Americans. This article focuses on George Klock, who was my nine times great uncle. He was notable for having one of the largest land disputes in the colonies with the British crown. Preston later published *Texture of Contact: European and Indian Settler Communities on the Frontiers of Iroquoia, 1667-1783*, where he discusses George Klock and his land disputes further. In this piece he explores how the Mohawks and colonists adapted their ways of life to co-exist.

*Imperial Entanglements: Iroquois Change and Persistence on the Frontiers of Empire* was written by Gail D. MacLeitch, a historian. In it, she speaks on how the lives of the Iroquois changed and adapted to the new economic and political factors during the eighteenth century. She also mentions their interactions with the German Palatines and how their actions affected life in the valley. George Klock and his land claims, which caused quite a stir between the Iroquois and the British Crown, are also explored in this work.

Eric Hinderaker authored *The Two Hendricks: Unraveling a Mohawk Mystery*, which is the most contemporary source that I reference. In it, Hinderaker separates the stories of two Mohawk chiefs, who were both known as "King Hendrick" by the British. History has remembered the stories of these Mohawk chiefs and morphed them into one person most likely because they shared the same first name once they were converted to the Dutch church. Both Hendricks interacted with the German Palatines, including the Klock family.

## Methodology

After looking at the prior academic research, I tried to find more specific information relating to my ancestors. I found references to many Klocks within these secondary sources mentioned above, but the next step is to find historical documents that pertain to them. I wanted to use these historical documents to paint a clearer picture of what the life was like for the Klocks living on what was then considered a frontier in colonial New York. I could not travel to upstate New York before this thesis was to be completed so I used online archives to access the necessary documents. Since I am unable to access the archives in person, there are limitations on what information I can include in this paper. As a result, there may be some gaps in the story of my ancestors. Historic records can also only offer so much information compared to people who have memories of certain events. Sadly, since I am researching ancestors who lived in the eighteenth century, I am unable to interview family members and ask them questions about the Klocks from this time period. Trying to uncover this family lineage is more difficult because I can't go to living family members and compare their stories with historical records. I will also examine the fingerprints that the Klocks left on American History. This family was affected by the French & Indian War and the American Revolution. There is a fortified homestead that still survives, called Fort Klock, which shows how much these wars affected their lives. I will use this vernacular building to help tell the story of my ancestors and examine how its preservation correlates to the preservation of my heritage.

This paper will be organized as a series of stories from my ancestor's lives instead of a conventional history paper. In order to better understand my ancestor's stories we need to understand who they were. Firstly, the origins and the struggles of the German Palatines who came to America during the eighteenth century will be explored. I also want to understand how my ancestors came to the colonies and what their journey to this "New World" was like. My research conducted on what life was like for the German Palatines living in the East and West Camps along the Hudson River in New York colony shall also be discussed. The next part of the Klock's story is how they settled and became pioneers in the Mohawk River Valley, owning land and becoming fur traders. Fort Klock was built in 1750 and I will explore what conditions would have led to my ancestors building a fortified homestead. The French & Indian War is the next historic event that greatly affected the Klock family. Within the next decade, the American Revolution was upon them. I will then discuss Fort Klock today and the state of its preservation.

**Origins of the German Palatines**

According to the National Park Service, German Palatines are those who "came from the Rhine Valley River region known as the 'Palatinate.' The name arose from the Roman word 'Palatine,' the title given to the ruling family of the area when it was part of the Holy Roman Empire."[2] This area of Central Europe is honored with the distinction of being known as the "cockpit of Europe". It was given this title during the Thirty Years' War (1618-1648), which was a fight between the Protestant and Catholic of the Holy Roman Empire. As the Thirty Years' War evolved, it became less about religion and more about who would ultimately govern Europe.[3] The Thirty Years' War forced many Protestant Palatines to flee their ancestral homeland, finding refuge in The Netherlands and England.[4] This led the English to devise a plan to send German Palatines across the Atlantic to the North Americans British colonies, many to New York colony.

## How the Klocks Came to British North America

The path my ancestors took to get to the New World is not evident in the examined historical records, but there are others that make up for missing information and provide valuable insights to the possible route the Klocks may have taken. While researching the Klocks, it became apparent that their surname was recorded in multiple ways. This is likely due to their German accent and the scribe's inability to clearly understand them. As a result, the Klocks name can also be found as Clock or Glock. According to Ancestry.com, the Klock surname may be a "habitational name from a house distinguished by the sign of a bell, Middle High German "glocke," Middle Dutch "clock." In some instances, this may also have been a metonymic occupational name for a bell maker or bell ringer."[5] The Klock coat of arms, which dates to circa 1450, depicts images of bells. In 1709, there were lists created of the Palatines that were in London. The names of Hendrick Klock or his wife Maria Margretha Schopferin did not appear on any of these lists. The last list was taken on June 5 of that year, so it is possible that the family came to London sometime between June and December of 1709, and then the ships carried the German Palatines to New York.

In December 1709, New York governor Robert Hunter decided to gather supplies that would be used by the Palatines.[6] Preparations for their transportation were also made. It was recorded "that all the Palatines embarked in December 1709 but did not start until April 10, 1710." [7] In Great Britain, a contract was written a few days before the Palatines set sail for New York that stated: "in consideration of the large sums advanced by the government 'toward the transporting, maintaining and settling' of the Palatines for their employment in the production of naval stores, the Palatines for themselves, their 'heirs' executors and administrators' contracted to settle on lands assigned to them by the government and continue resident upon those lands. On no account or manner of pretense were the Palatines to quit or desert without leave of the governor. They agreed to employ their utmost power and that of their respective families in the 'production and manufacturing of all manner of naval stores.' It was further agreed 'that as soon as we shall have made good and repaid to her Majesty, her heirs and successors, out of the produce of our labors in the manufactures we are employed in, the full sum or sums of money in which we already are or shall become indebted to her Majesty.'"[8] The contract also stated that each person was to be granted 40 acres of land that would be "free from all taxes, quit rents or other manner of services for seven years."[9] A length of time was not specified for the Palatines indentured servitude to the British government, but it was evident that they were to produce and "manufacture naval stores until the profits had not only paid their expenses, but also repaid the Queen for their transportation and settlement."[10]

The migration of German Palatines to America in 1709 was the most significant of the colonial period. The living conditions aboard these ships was horrifying: "They were on board ship for six long months and the sufferings of the Palatines were terrible...the people were closely packed in the ships. Many of them suffered from the foul odor and vermin; some below deck could neither get fresh air nor see the light of day. Under such conditions the younger children died in great numbers...Good healthy food was not provided and its lak no doubt added to the general unhealthy conditions. Soon the fleet was ravaged by ship-fever. Modern science has traced this maladyn, now known as typhus and recognized as more deadly than typhoid, to such carriers as infected fleas and body lice. Crowded in those foul holds with little or no provision for the most elementary sanitation, the immigrants were decimated by this dread disease. From the misery indeed, the disease took on a rather sad distinction since it became known to the doctors of that day as the 'Palatine fever'."[11]

When the Palatines arrived in New York in the summer of 1710 it became apparent to them that the English Colony of New York in which they now resided was not the paradise that was described in the golden books that they had been exposed to in Germany. When they first got to New York they weren't even allowed in the city due to the large number of Palatines who had contracted "Palatine fever." "The New York City Council protested the arrival of 2,500 disease-laden newcomers within their jurisdiction and demanded the Germans stay in tents on Nutten (now Governors) Island offshore. Typhus continued to decimate the emigrants. Altogether about 470 Palatines died on the voyage from England and during their first month in New York."[12]

The names of the 847 families who survived the perilous journey across the Atlantic Ocean are found in the Hunter Subsistence Lists. These were lists taken from 1710 to 1712 to record Governor Hunter's payment for the subsistence of the Palatine families.[13] The records in which the Klocks first appeared in, after reaching the colonies, are Governor Hunter's Ration Lists. My nine times great-grandfather Hendrick Klock (1663-1760) is listed in these records. His name was recorded as "Henrich Glock."[14] On the list from June 30, 1710, Hendrick was recorded as having one person over 10 years old and three under 10 years old in his family.[15]

One of the locations that the English were interested in settling the German Palatines was an area known as Schoharie. This land was occupied by the Native Americans, specifically the Mohawk tribe, and at first, they didn't allow the Englishmen to survey the land. Governor Hunter believed that the Mohawk had no right to this land and on August 22, 1710, he met with a man who was known as Tejonihokarawa. He was one of the "four Indian kings" who traveled to London in 1710 and met with Queen Ann and other dignitaries. Tejonihokarawa told Governor Hunder, "We are told that the great queen of Great Britain had sent a considerable number of People with you Excy to settle upon the land called the Skohere, which was a great surprise to us, and we were much Disatisfyd at the news, in Regard the Land belongs to us.... Nevertheless since Your Excellcy has been pleased to desire the said land for Christian settlements, we are willing and do now Surrender...to the Queen...for Ever all that tract of Land Called Skohere."[16] This land lacked pine trees in the area that could be used for making tar which would in turn be used to produce naval stores. As a result, the German Palatines didn't settle in Schoharie.

"On 29 September 1710, Governor Hunter entered into an agreement with Robert Livingston, Commissioner of Indian Affairs, to purchase a tract of 6,000 acres on the east side of the Hudson for the purpose of settling Palatines there to manufacture naval stores." Many of the German Palatines went up the river in October 1710 to clear the ground and build huts. "Gradually, small, distinct settlements appear at East Camp called Hunterstown, Queensbury, Annsbury, and Haysbury; the villages on the west side of the Hudson were Elizabeth Town, George Town and New Town."[17] The Klock family were not found on the census of the camps, so it is believed that they resided in the East Camp because no census record for that place has been discovered yet. In 1717, Ulrich Simmendinger, who was an immigrant, returned to Germany and "published this brief account of the migration and the names of those Palatine families still living in New York." [18] The Klocks are recorded as "Klock, Henrick, (h) w. Maria Margretha & 4 ch". [19] In the key of this record (h) stands for Queensbury or Qünsberg as it would have been known in German. This was the village in the East Camp that the

Klock family would have resided in. This record tells us that Hendrick and his wife Maria Margretha had four children, one of them being my eight times great-grandfather, Hendrick Klock (Jr.) who was the eldest child of Hendrick Klock (Sr.). The first child born to Hendrick and Maria Margretha in the New World was Johannes on October 30, 1711.[20] He would be the first in the family to not know any other life than the one his family lived in the countryside of New York colony.

The German Palatine's discontent for their status, which was borderline serfdom, continued to grow and they demanded the lands that were promised to them in London. A rebellion was put down by Governor Hunter. The Palatines were disarmed and put "under the command of overseers and a Court of Palatine Commissioners, who treated them again as 'the Queen's hired servants.'" They also began to notice that they were given inferior food supplies.[21] By 1711, politics in England began to have a great effect on the fate of the German Palatines that resided along the Hudson River in New York. The Whigs party, who were largely supportive of the Palatine settlement in New York, were replaced in office by the Tories, who set out to disassemble the 1709 Whig project.[22] On June 4, 1711, the House of Commons presented this statement to Queen Anne: "We cannot omit taking notice to Your Majesty, of another Extraordinary instance in which the publick Money has been apply'd, by bringing over the Poor Palatines to Inhabit and Settle themselves in this Kingdom. This was not only an Extravagant and unreasonable Expense in itself, but many other ways uneasy and grievons to Your People; for as it was visible that such Numbers of Necessiwous and useless Foreigners must unavoidably ten to the Encrease and Opression of the Poor of this Kingdom."[23] The House of Commons investigation that ensued, caused Governor Hunter to lose the financial support that was used to help support the German Palatines in colonial New York. The British government fell through on their promises and the Palatines were left to suffer their own fate. Hunter had to stop providing food for the Palatines in September 1712. Reverend Johann Friedreich Hager wrote a letter in July 1713 in which he described the horror of which had now become reality for the Palatines: "The misery of these poor Palatines I every day behold has thrown me into such a fit of melancholy that I much fear a sickness. There has been a great famine among them this winter, and odes hold still, in so much that they boil grass, and the children eat the leaves of the trees. Such amongst them have most suffered of hunger as are advanced in years and too weak to go out laboring."[24]

The luck of the Palatines started to look up in 1715 when a Naturalization Act was passed "and all persons of foreign birth inhabitants of New York in 1715 and Protestants were naturalized, provided they took the oath of Allegiance and Supremacy and subscribed to the Test and the Abjuration Oath."[25] Many of the Palatines decided to take this opportunity to become naturalized. On October 11, 1715, there was a Hendrick Klock naturalized in Albany and on January 3, 1716, a Hans Hendrick Clock was also naturalized in Albany. I believe that these men were my nine- and eight-times great-grandfathers respectively. It seems that the one recorded as "Hans Hendrick Clock" was my eight times great grandfather. On later records his name is recorded as Hendrick Klock, but perhaps on the naturalization papers the father and son's names were recorded differently to help differentiate between the two.[26]

Between 1713 and 1718 many of the Palatines would relocate.[27] After the Palatines left the tar camps some experienced the first winter living in caves before they could build more appropriate accommodations.[28] Since they were not permitted to bring with them the tools they were assigned in the tar camps it took some time for them to find the appropriate tools needed to build their homesteads.[29] Many of the Palatines moved to Schoharie and "were totally dependent upon their Mohawk neighbors for basic necessities." [30] The Palatines convinced the Mohawks to sell them the land and after buying the land the "the Palatines were called upon in 1715 to purchase, lease or vacate their land. Hunter claimed in 1720 that at his instance favorable terms were extended to the Palatines, offering the land free from all rent for ten years, and after that on only a very moderate quit-rent. They refused and grew violent." [31]

When other colonists with secured purchases from the Mohawks and government patents began to settle on the land in Schoharie the Palatines began to destroy the homesteads of these newly arrived colonists and in some instances beat them. The Palatines believed that the land was theirs. In 1718, the Palatines sent representatives to London to ask for justice. These deputies were robbed by pirates and when they reached London they were imprisoned for debt. "By that time Hunter himself had returned to London to recoup his fortune. He falsely claimed that the Palatines had taken possession of lands in Schoharie already granted to others...His suggestion that they be removed to other lands on the frontier were adopted." Governor William Burnet, Hunter's successor, was ordered to move the Palatines to suitable lands.[32]

How the Klock family ended up from the tar camps to the Mohawk River Valley isn't very clear, but the area where they ended up settling in the upper valley region became a Palatine haven in the eighteenth century.[33] It is likely that they may have traveled with other German Palatines and settled in Schoharie for a few years, and then once the Palatines were ordered to be moved to the frontier lands, they ended up in the Mohawk River Valley. During the eighteenth century, the Mohawk River Valley was considered a frontier between indigenous peoples, British and French colonists. "European and Indian communities were strongly bound together by a network of personal, cultural, religious, economic, and military ties."[34]

The Klocks resided in the Mohawk River Valley by 1721 because my nine times great-grandmother Maria Margretha Schopferin Klock is said to have died in Stone Arabia that year.[35] In 1723, "300 palatines moved from schoharie to the settlements of stone arabia and the german flats, on or near the mohawk river."[36] So perhaps the Klocks were some of the Palatines to move to the area. Stone Arabia is the area located along the North side of the Mohawk River and it is coincidentally beside the land that the Klocks would later permanently settle. When the Klocks first came to the Mohawk Valley they appeared to have good relations with their Mohawk neighbors and regularly traded with them. Members of the Klock family even learned to speak the Mohawk language.[37] The family's relations with the Mohawks appear to have been well enough to have a familial connection. "When the Board of Trade wrote in favor of the Palatine emigration in 1709, it noted its belief that the Palatines would 'in process of time by intermarrying with the neighboring Indians (as the French do) . . . be Capable [of] rendering very great Service to Her Majesty's Subjects.'"[38] The British understood that by intermarrying with the Mohawks, the colonists could have better trading and political relations.

In 1727, my eight times great-grandparents were married in Germantown, New York. Hendrick Klock (1693-1759), the oldest son of the pioneer of Hendrick Klock (1668-1760), married Jacomyntie, who was Mohawk.[39] This marriage may have occurred because some of the Klock family wanted to become fur traders. When a European colonist married a Native American, it allowed them to trade with the indigenous peoples.

According to Jacomyntie's memorial on Findagrave.com, she was the daughter of Tejonihokarawa, the Mohawk Chief previously mentioned. It is also said that her father-in-law, Hendrick Klock, was good friends with Tejonihokarawa.[40] Historian Eric Hinderaker, says there was only one known daughter of Tejonihokarawa named Lysbet, and after speaking with him he was skeptical to believe that Jacomyntie Klock could have been a daughter of Tejonihokarawa.[41] One theory is that the English didn't accept indigenous polygamist marriages as "legitimate," so Tejonihokarawa could have had more than one wife, and thus children with each wife.

On March 8, 1722, the Harrison Patent was granted. It contains 12,000 acres, including nearly all of what is now known as the town of St. Johnsville. To the southern border of this patent lies the Mohawk River. To the east lies the patent of Stone Arabia.[42] On a 1754 copy of the Harrison Patent, four Klock men are shown as owning plats on this land. To the north of the Harrison Patent lies the Klock Purchase, which is also referred to as the Klock-Nellis patent, granted December 21, 1754. On this plat ten men of the Klock family owned land.[43] Once the German Palatines began to settle along the Mohawk River, many of "their log and stone houses dotted clearings in the wilderness."[44] These settlers bore the brunt of aggression from the French, Mohawk, and Loyalists in the wars to come. "Substantial stone structures afforded refuge to owners and neighbors, alike, at the time of savage raids. With log palisades and, perhaps also, with a small blockhouse, these places later came to be referred to as 'forts.'"[45] These forts were the architecture of fear and security on the frontier.

In 1750, Johannes Klock built what would become known as Fort Klock. This structure lies less than a mile east of the town of St. Johnsville, replacing Johannes's earlier abode that stood on the same site.[46] This property is located on plat number 11 of the

Harrison Patent that was previously mentioned.[47] The mason builder of this fortified homestead was Willem Pick. Fort Klock "is a very strongly built stone house resting on the solid rock, from which emerges a living spring."[48] It is a vernacular "L" shaped building that is two and a half stories with a cellar (Figure 4.2).

The walls of Fort Klock are over two feet thick and are loopholed on every side for defense, creating musket holes built into the walls.[49] Johannes, like other family members, was engaged in the Mohawk Valley fur trade. Fort Klock was used as a trading post and was the center of his business.[50] Its location along the King's Highway brought many past this site. Fortified homesteads were common in the Mohawk Valley during the eighteenth century. Two of Johannes's brothers, George and Jacob, were said to also have fortified homes.[51] People living in this area decided to build in this way because their lives were under constant threat from violence on the frontier.

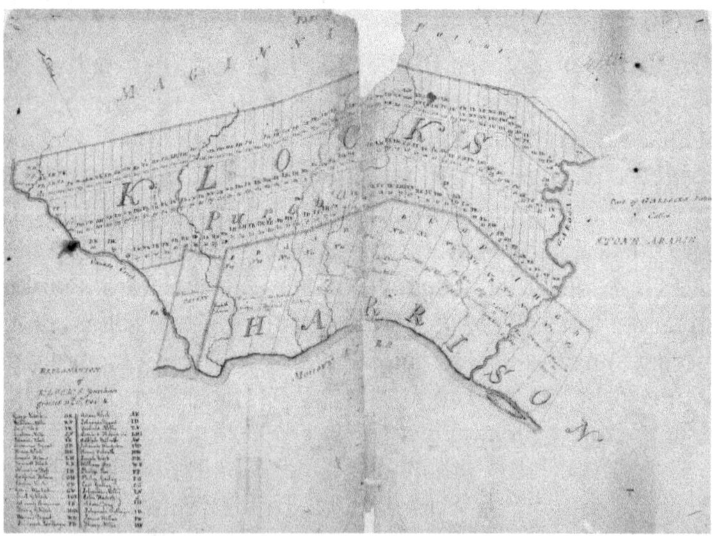

Figure 4.2: Map of Klock's Purchase, Magin's Tract and Harrison Tract. Map #865A. New York State Archives. New York State

Engineer and Surveyor. Survey maps of lands in New York State, ca.1711-1913. Series A0273-78, Map #865A.

## The French & Indian War

With the start of the French & Indian War came Sir William Johnson, who became the Superintendent of Indian Affairs in 1755. He came to the colony in the 1740s to manage his uncle's estate in the Mohawk Valley and he soon started trading with the Mohawks. The "English political and military leaders recognized Johnson's talents in working with Indians." While he "appointed as Superintendent of Indian Affairs and was given a dual military commission as 'Colonel of the Six Nations' and Major General of provincial forces."[52] At the time, Johnson was arguably the most important Indian official on the continent and was a direct representative of the British Crown.[53]

"The Seven Years' War was a defining moment in the relationships among Klock, the Palatines, and their Mohawk and Oneida neighbors. George Klock was a central negotiator in Palatine and Oneida efforts to create what Cadwallader Colden called a 'private Neutrality: between their communities during the war's upheaval…The Germans also had little desire to become involved in what they saw as an English war."[54] He was one of the many sons of the elder Hendrick Klock. He held many complex and sophisticated diplomatic meetings with the Mohawks and Palatine settlers during this time. "Klock 'Frequently called, and held private meetings with the Indians, at which he and some other of ye. Germans living in that quarter have endeavored by false tales, and artfully insinuating to create differences, and misunderstandings, between the Army Inhabitants and Indians.' But far more than falsehood and artifice were involved in those private meetings."[55]

In November 1757, the French & Indian War came close to home for the Klocks and the Palatines of the Mohawk River Valley. "Nearly two hundred Mississaugas and Canadian Iroquois and around sixty-five French marines and militia embarked on an expedition against New York. Their target was a prosperous settlement called German Flatts in the upper Mohawk Valley." [56] German Flatts is located twenty miles away from where the Klock family was, near St. Johnsville. "German Flatts was defended by a substantial star-shaped redoubt called Fort Herkimer and a series of five blockhouses in the surrounding settlements." The French forces bypassed the fort and attacked the Palatine settlement directly. Many were killed while more were taken captive and many of the built structures such as homes, barns, and outhouses were burnt to ashes.[57]

While the Palatines were being attacked by the French and their Native American allies, this did not include the Mohawk and the Oneida tribes around them. "The Palatines communicated to the Oneidas their resentment of 'the ill treatment they receive from the English, meaning the Troops, who past and repast that Way, as well as from those posted there.'"[58] The Palatine settlers living in the Mohawk River Valley "not only participated in this thriving Iroquois trade but conducted their own diplomacy, separate from the British government."[59] In 1760, the elder Hendrick Klock died at the age of 91 or 92. His tombstone still stands. It reads "HERE LEY HK 1760". He was buried on his son George's land in an area where numerous numbers of the family would be buried, which would later become known as Klock Cemetery.[60] It was well known that there was bad blood between Johnson and the Klocks.[61]

Johnson held a great disdain for George Klock, who can be described as "the black sheep of a respectable Palatine family." [62] According to Preston, both of these men were conniving individuals who were so similar that they hated each other with great passion.[63] By 1761, "Johnson and Klock came to blows over the lands surrounding Canajoharie." [64] George became "jealousies and suspicions lingered long after peace returned to the Mohawk Valley, land controversies in colonial New York tended to smolder for decades. One of the most hotly contested land deals of the eighteenth century was over the 1731 Canajoharie Patent that encompassed the Canajoharie Mohawks' settlements and planting grounds on the south side of the Mohawk River." [65] Klock unearthed this patent and caused a political stir with the Mohawks and Sir William Johnson.

"The Canajoharie Mohawks were particularly aggrieved because Klock's actions threatened to overturn the harmonious and symbolic relationships that they had forged with other German farmers: their tenants...Mohawks had occasionally invited trustworthy colonists - usually families like the Klocks who came to them in poverty - to use and farm their lands. A Number of Germans became tenants and paid rents such as corn or wheat to Indian, no colonial, landlords; Klock, in fact, was the leader in initially helping 'to Settle the Rent w$^{h}$. The Tenants pay to the Ind$^{s}$' and he 'kept Rent Rool thereof.'"[66] With Klock laying claim to the lands that the Canajoharie Village set on, the tenants would be paying dues to him and not the Mohawks. This caused there to be a question of authority in the Mohawk Valley. Whose authority was supreme in this situation, George Klock, the Canajoharie Mohawks, or Sir William Johnson?

To make greater legitimacy to his claims, "Klock needed to obtain requisite Indian deeds affirming the original purchase of Canajoharie lands. His modus operandi in these purchases was to get individual Mohawk men or women drunk and then coax, bribe, or force them to sign deeds affirming land sales over which they had no individual authority." [67] The methodology that Klock used to better support his claim also came under fire. Johnson described George Klock as "so designing [and] litigious a Rogue, that there is not a man in the Country would choose to have a penny dealing with him." [68] While this description may hold some truth his actions did cause a divide between many of his neighbors, even his own family. "His brother Jacob swore an affidavit that exposed Klock's fraudulent practices and affirmed that the Indians would not part with the lands that George claimed. Jacob also complained that he was 'frequently troubled, and Disturbed, day and night, and Obliged to get up at all Hours of the night to let in the Drunken Indians' coming from his brother's house."[69] Many of the Klock family members lived within walking distance to each other. "William Johnson once spent a sleepless night at Klock's brother's house nearby for 'by their Singing dancing & other noise I was disturbed during the whole night."[70]

It is questionable how much of Johnson's disdain for George Klock stems from the "British elites' cultural distain for the 'boorish, nay brutish disposition of the country people'". It appears that "Johnson feared the rise of a German landlord with great influence among the Iroquois."[71] "Klock was without question a persuasive, knowledgeable, and skillful negotiator who had some support among the Iroquois. A small band of around twenty Iroquois men and women- 'The Conajoharie Ind.^s who are Ury [George] Klocks Party' - thought enough of Klock to separate from the main settlements at Canajoharie and move to his fam on the river's north side. The natives who were 'all ways living at his house' also supported his claims, resented Johnson, and bickered with their kin at the main settlements." [72] Johnson did everything in his power to block George Klock from obtaining any land. He "offered land to colonial officials like Goldsbrow Banyar and surveyor Alexander Colden" to help him ensure that Klock was not able to expand his land ownership. "Before the American Revolution, Klock was never able to receive letters patent for tracts that he had legally licensed, purchased, and surveyed between 1754 and 1760."[73]

To better understand this situation and the relationship between George and Johnson let us examine their similarities. It is believed that the main reason Johnson was so upset with George's actions is because he was after the same land and fearful that he would be replaced as the man with the most influence on Native Americans in New York colony.[74] Johnson always depicted himself as an ally to the Mohawks, but in reality he was "a land owner, developer, and broker" and he also "contributed to the Mohawk's diminishing land base."[75] "As early as 1750, Johnson was interested in patenting 10,000 acres of land around Canajoharie and solicited Governor Clinton's involvement and approval. In 1761 the Canajoharie Mohawks entrusted Johnson with a large tract of their remaining lands on the north side of the Mohawk River, between East and West Canada Creeks. They intended this gift as a deed in trust, to protect and preserve their lands from colonial encroachments."[76] While the Mohawks may have wanted Johnson to help them preserve this land, it was Johnson's plan to "settle a number of people on the land directly."[77] "His gift from the Mohawks was transformed into a royal land grant from George III in 1769 that encompassed some 100,000 acres of prime Mohawk land. Johnson and the thirty-eight other grantees then subdivided and began settling the lands with Europeans."[78]

At the end of the French & Indian War, the Royal Proclamation of 1763 was made by the British to appease Native Americans, by checking the encroachment of colonists on their lands. The royal proclamation prohibited colonial expansion West of the Appalachian Mountains.[79] The end of this war "symbolized the beginning of racial violence and the end of earlier coexistence"[80] between the Mohawks and the German Palatines that could be seen across the frontier. In 1763 and 1768, "the New York government brought two separate suits against Klock…but both prosecutions were unsuccessful."[81] Even though up to this point George had not been prosecuted, Johnson still made it his life's mission. In 1773, George made a "voyage to London with his Mohawk associate." George made this transatlantic journey to plead his case with a petition to the king. He "may have undertaken his voyage for both principal and profit, by 'Exhibiting [the] Mohawk' as a show' in London's coffeehouses and taverns."[82] The best part of this story is that the vessel that George and his Canajoharie companion sailed on was named *Sir William Johnson*. It was a "two-masted, square-sailed snow, launched in 1772 and owned by the London merchant John Blackburn… Klock's voyage and his choice of an appropriately named sailing vessel were intentional acts of defiance of Johnson's authority as royally appointed superintendent of Indian Affairs."[83] Johnson died in 1774 and did not get to see George punished in any way.

**The American Revolution**

On May 21, 1775, a dozen men of the Mohawk Valley gathered together to create the Palatine Committee of Correspondence, which would become "known as the Committee of Safety and to govern the valley in their own way until a stable government was finally formed in 1777, met at the home of Philip Fox opposite old Palatine Church and adopted the following resolution: "As we abhor a state of slavery we do join and unite together under all the ties of religion, honor, justice and love of our country, never to become slaves and to defend our freedom with our lives and fortunes."[84]

Two days prior to this, on May 19, 1775, the same men that would later create the committee held "a long dissertation setting forth their grievances they closed with the solemn resolution 'To be Free or Die.' These declarations were signed and published by the men of the Palatine Committee, the first to form themselves into such a body, and they gave their lives liberally at Oriskany." One of the dozen men to sign this declaration and form this committee was Jacob Klock.[85] The actions of these men in the Mohawk Valley took place over a year before the final document of the Declaration of Independence on July 4, 1776. Here at the Old Palatine Church, these men banded themselves together and called for liberty or death.[86] "Committees of correspondence were emergency provisional governments set up in the 13 American colonies in response to British policies leading up to the Revolutionary War. The exchange of ideas, information and debate between different committees of correspondence helped organize and mobilize patriotic resistance in communities throughout the colonies and built the foundations for the Continental Congress."[87]

These Palatines compared themselves to slaves of the British. While they lived lives that bordered on serfdom in the tar camps decades earlier, during the 1770s some Palatines in the Mohawk Valley enslaved Africans. Colonel Jacob Klock was one of the enslavers. In his 1798 will he left his enslaved to two of his granddaughters. "I give and bequeath unto said Eva Klock my negro wench Sarah and her two son Hank and George and also my negro child Margaret to her heirs and assign forever. I give and bequeath to Anna Dysslin…my negro child called Sarah to her heirs and assigns forever."[88] After Johnson's death in 1774, "his son, Sir John, succeeded to the bulk of his vast possessions in the most troublous times of New York's history. He owed everything to the Crown and nothing to the people."[89] As a result, he took up arms for the British and became a Loyalists.

During this point in history there was "a line of frontier settlements stretched westward along the Mohawk Valley sixty-five miles from Schenectady to

German Flats. Agriculturally rich, the valley served as a major breadbasket for the Patriot cause. Its white population of 15,000 settlers provided a militia force of about 2,500 men."[90] The chance of an invasion from Canada began to increase and settlers of the Mohawk Valley "began erecting a series of military posts and also built stockades around a number of stone dwellings and churches until a total of some 24 strong post guarded the valley. The purpose of these fortified private houses was to provide places of safety where neighboring settlers could seek refuge when bands of raiding Indians and Tories swept through the valley."[91] During the American Revolution, Fort Klock was said to have welcomed many guests, but not in the normal way. It was frequently used during this time period as a place of refuge by many of the locals and neighboring families.

Sixteen men in the Klock family were involved in the Revolutionary War.[92] Johannes Klock, who built Fort Klock, "fought as a member of the Tryon County militia at the Battle of Orinsky August 6, 1777."[93] My seven times great-grandfather Johannes Klock (1730-1815) was a private in Captain Christopher Fox's Company, which was regiment led by Colonel Jacob Klock, the latter being his uncle.[94] Jacob Klock was in a significant positions to be involved in correspondence with General George Washington regarding field instructions (Figure 4.3). This may have been in response to "scalping parties of Canadian Indians and Tories began in the Mohawk valley about 1778 and continued up to 1783, when a peace treaty was signed." [95] So many of these incidents took place that it is impossible to know how many of them occurred and the records have not been preserved. When the nearby town of Ephrathah was attacked, "two Indians of the raiding party shot and killed a girl named Rickard, as she was driving home cows near Fort Klock.... Hearing the shot, George Klock came running out with his gun and as the Indians made for the girl's body to scalp it, he fired, and they made for the woods and disappeared."[96]

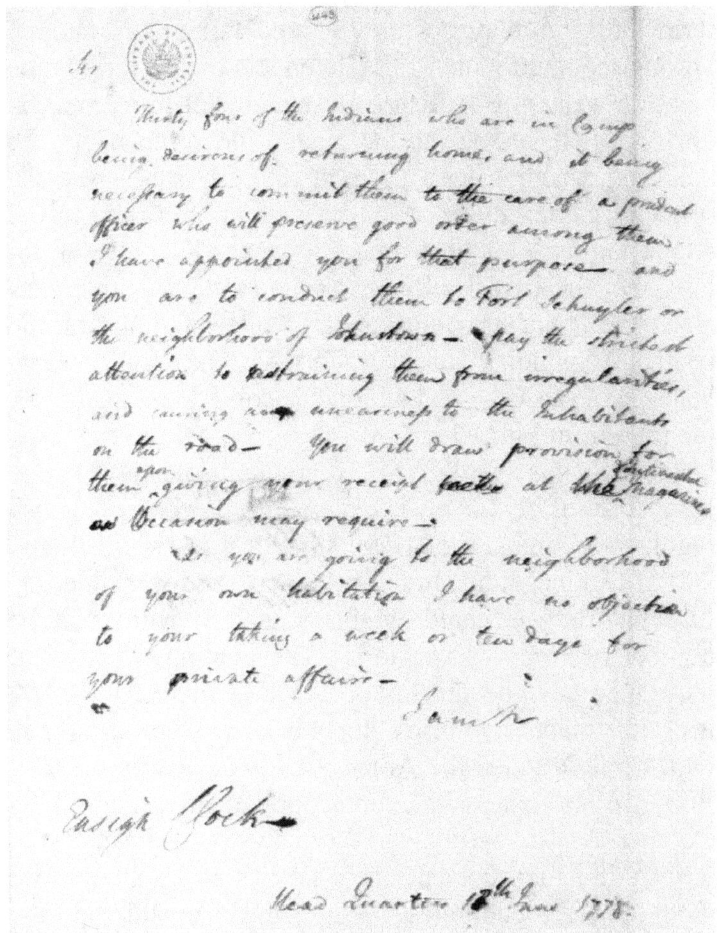

Sir

Thirty four of the Indians who are in Camp being desirous of returning home, and it being necessary to commit them to the care of a prudent officer who will preserve good order among them I have appointed you for that purpose — and you are to conduct them to Fort Schuyler or the neighborhood of Johnstown — pay the strictest attention to restraining them from irregularities, and causing no uneasiness to the Inhabitants on the road — You will draw provision for them upon giving your receipt at the Continental Magazines as Occasion may require —

As you are going to the neighborhood of your own habitation I have no objection to your taking a week or ten days for your private affairs —

I am Sr

Ensign Klock

Head Quarters 13th June 1778.

Figure 4.3: Correspondence: George Washington to Jacob I. Klock, June 13, 1778. Donald Jackson and Dorothy Twohig, eds. *The Diaries of George Washington,* 6 Volumes (Charlottesville: University Press of Virginia, 1976-79); a series of The Papers of George Washington. Copyright 1976-79 by the Rector and Visitors of University of Virginia. Used by permission of the publisher.

"Bands of Iroquois warriors and Tories destroyed houses, barns, and crops in the vicinity of Fort Klock on April 18, 1779, August 2, 1780, and October 18-19, 1780.

The third attack resulted in the Battle of Klock's Field."[97] Fort Klock overlooks the battle of Klocks Field from October 19, 1780, which happened on the Klock's farm with neighboring families and farmer militiamen. During the battle, one of the defenders took a long range bead on a passing British officer and shot him from his horse, which, strange to say, came galloping up to the palisade, where it was secured. On its back "was the officer's camp kettle, which became an heirloom in the Klock family."[98] John Crouse, Johannes Klock's son in-law, shot the British officer. At the battle a woman was also struck by a stray musket ball while standing near the southeast window of the Fort. [99] The Klock farm belonged to George and Colonel Jacob Klock, just down the road from Fort Klock.

At this battle "Sir John Johnson, lead three companies of his Loyalist 'Greens,' a company of British regulars, a company of Hessian jaegers or rifleman, and 200 of Colonel John Butler's Rangers" and was aided by "Joseph Brant, feared Mohawk chief…with a large number of Iroquois warriors." The combined forces of these men have been estimated to have ranged from 800 to 1,500 men.[100] Johnson and his men were resting in Klock's field when the American forces, led by General Robert Van Renessaler, came upon them at sunset on October 19. The patriots are estimated to have had 700 to 900 militia men present. This Patriot band, along with their Oneida comrades, began their pursuit of the Loyalists after they burned the nearby town of Stone Arabia to the ground, and they followed them westward along the Mohawk River.[101] The American victory at the Battle of Klock's field put an end to Sir John Johnson's raid on the Mohawk Valley.

Three years after the Battle of Klock's Field, the American Revolution came to an end through the Treaty of Paris, signed on September 3, 1783. Peace finally came to the beleaguered people of the Mohawk

Valley.[102] "After six years of constant warfare, condition in the Mohawk Valley were far different: more than 700 homes had been burned, the white population was reduced to 5,000 and its militia to 800 men. Tens of thousands of people had fled to Canada or out of the valley, hundreds had been killed or taken prisoner. It was the privately fortified structures such as Fort Klock that enabled the 5,000 settlers still living in the Mohawk Valley in 1781 to survive until the end of hostilities."[103] Fort Klock was one of the select few structures that survived the war. "Jacob Klock's regiment of New-York militia, [was] allowed a pension, at the rate of five dollars per month"[104] from August 20, 1777. It was rare for men to earn money for their service in the Revolutionary War. Many were offered land as compensation. With the Americans victory in the War for Independence, George Klock was able to gain full legal rights to some of the Canajoharie lands that had long been disputed over.[105]

**State of Preservation**

For well over two centuries Fort Klock has stood. Until the mid-twentieth century the structure was owned and occupied by Klock descendants. It is currently owned by Fort Klock Historic Restoration and the structure was listed on the National Register of Historic Places in 1972.[106] Fort Klock is currently a house museum that is open for tours during the summer months and the Fort Klock Historic Restoration has done a fantastic job restoring the historic structure and maintaining it over the years. Fort Klock is one of only two eighteenth-century fortified homesteads in New York state, that are listed on the National Register of Historic Places. Both are located in Montgomery County.[107] The other "fortified homestead" is Fort Johnson that was the home of the previously mentioned Sir William Johnson. Johannes Klock designed his homestead to appeal to Dutch and German settlers that would rather trade with someone other than the British. Stylistically it echoes the vernacular buildings that these colonists would have been more familiar with. Fort Johnson was built as a status symbol and would have been more familiar to the British colonial elite. During the American Revolution, it had a wooden palisade put up around it and it earned the name "Fort" Johnson.[108] While Fort Klock also once had a wooden palisade surrounding, it was also built with musket holes in the walls on each side of the homestead.[109] One could argue that Fort Klock is the only true eighteenth century fortified homestead in New York state because that was its intended purpose when it was built. Fort Klock was listed on the National Register of Historic Places for its relation to commerce, military, and the fur trade.[110]

The houses of George and Jacob Klock that sat a short distance down the road from Fort Klock along the King's Highway no longer exist. Currently, there are multiple buildings on the land that used to belong to the brothers. On the site of Colonel Jacob Klock's home, there is a boulder with a tablet laid into it describing the site's historic significance.[111] Behind the site of George Klock's homestead lies the Klock Church Burial ground. There also appears to be another Klock Cemetery just down the road. Both have multiple headstones that are still intact. There also appear to be records of those buried there with no headstone. This is most likely due to the fact they may have not been able to afford a stone headstone and opted for a wooden marker. Wooden markers were often made to look like headboards, connecting to the term "rest in peace". Wooden markers would explain why there are no stone grave markers in place, because the material would have deteriorated.

It does not appear that Fort Klock is in any imminent danger for the foreseeable future. Very few fortified homesteads from this era are left and that helps protect this historic site. While I do not believe that this historic structure could ever intentionally be demolished, stranger things have happened. New York is known for its harsh winters, and at this point in time, it seems that the only danger Fort Klock could be in would be due to inclement weather that could possibly cause damage to the historic structure. Fort Klock Historic Restoration hosts a large number of events each season to get the community involved and educate them about the history of the surrounding area.

Fort Klock is currently being displayed as a house museum. The interior of the house is set up to reflect what it may have looked like during the mid to late eighteenth century. There aren't really any displays that depict or tell the history of the German Palatines or the Klock family. There are also long-term concerns of weathering to be mindful of. The Fort Klock Historic Restoration also owns other buildings on the property that could possibly be used to better interpret the history. At Fort Klock there is an old cheese house and a barn. The cheese house is used to house the interpreter of the fort. The organization also owns a nearby blacksmith shop and a historic schoolhouse.

**Lineage Forgotten**

This part of my family lineage had been forgotten until I started doing research in the early 2010s. I am related to the Klocks through my father's side of the family. Looking on the paternal side of my family tree you come across my two times great-grandfather Raymond Edward Rowsam (1884-1976). His mother was Clara E. Edick (1862-1930), my three times great grandmother. She was the daughter of my four great-grandparents, Anson Edick (1822-1906) and Magdalena Elizabeth Klock (1829-1886). The Edick (Ittig) family were also German Palatines who made the journey over to New York with the Klocks in 1709. Anson Edick was also descended from another German Palatine family, the Empie family who also made the journey in 1709, who he was connected through his paternal grandmother, Elizabeth Empie (1774-1847).

I often wonder why this history was forgotten by my family. The Klocks and other German Palatine families we are related to all settled along the Mohawk River below the Adirondack mountains. Over time, my ancestors moved west of the Adirondacks. Perhaps this history was forgotten because my family moved away from the area. It also occurred to me that this part of our family history was not remembered because of the female connection of Clara Edick and her mother Magdalena Klock. If the connection had been directly through my paternal line this history may have been better remembered. It is amazing how easy it is for the past to be forgotten, including our own. If have to strive to remember it in order to teach future generations about what happened.

**Conclusion**

Completing this chapter has helped me learn more about my heritage that was previously unknown to me. This is something that I can share with my family and future generations to come. I want the information to be available to my descendants, so they won't have to do the research that I had to. I don't want this history to be forgotten again. It is mind boggling to me that I am the twelfth generation of this family line that has lived in the Americas. As a child I never imagined that my ancestors had played roles in the founding of our nation because I did not have access to resources that would have helped me realize otherwise. Conducting this research has caused me to have a sense of *anemoia*, the feeling of nostalgia for a time you've never known. This part of my family history is very important to me even though I will never be able to experience what life was like for my ancestors. I have discovered the tools and records that will help me to imagine them. I have never researched my genealogy so in depth to the point where I created a narrative that told the story of what my ancestors' lives were like. I am sure that none of my ancestors were perfect people and I have provided evidence of this within this paper. The history of this family is intertwined with the history of the British North American colonies and the United States. By better understanding their story one can better appreciate the history of this country. The Klock "family's experience, at least, challenges the general sense in current histories that frontier violence in the Seven Years' War and the American Revolution foreclosed on the peaceful relations between Indians and Europeans."[112] We may have forgotten their names and deeds, but it is our duty to seek to remember them again.

# Chapter 5: A Hellene in Hell's Kitchen: Greek Perspectives of Ethnicity and Homeland in Twentieth Century America

By Noah Sigalas

All throughout grade school, I didn't know who I was—not just in the vague listless sense that all teenage boys experience adolescent identity instability, but on a deep, personal level. What was I, ethnically speaking? What did it mean that I was one ethnicity or another and not just "American" like a lot of my schoolmates thought of themselves? Throughout school, kids took the liberty of giving me a label that they thought fit. I was misidentified with all kinds of groups: people thought that I was Chinese (?!), Mexican, Amish, Mormon, Muslim, you name it. I was probably associated with every group that my classmates were aware of. My classmates didn't know who or "what" I was—only that I didn't seem to fit in with their general notions of "Americanness." As funny and confusing as the guesses they made, in truth I too had no idea who or what I was or into which category I was supposed to neatly fit.

It wasn't until I got a little older (7-9 years old) that I started to listen to the stories that my father and grandfather told me about my *papu* Γεώργιος Κωνσταντίνος Σιγάλας (Yiorgios Konstantinos Sigalas—also known as: George Constantine Sigalas, which is how I will refer to him in the remainder of this paper, but I will mostly be using the familiar Papu which means "grandpa"). From his experiences as a Greek immigrant in the early twentieth century, I began to form an understanding of myself as someone of Greek heritage. I was utterly captivated by the stories my father told me about Papu's exploits in Hell's Kitchen, New York City from the 1910s through the 1930s, and how he had to struggle to make something of himself, since many Americans at the time looked down on immigrants. I was inspired by his extreme toughness and stubbornness in the face of insult, intimidation, threat of violence, and actual violence, that was standard early twentieth century fare for people of my great grandfather's ethnic background and social status. I really appreciated the hard work that he did to make a living as an automobile mechanic in gang-controlled Hell's Kitchen. What was perhaps more relevant to my struggle was thinking about how Papu was, in some respects, the progenitor of my family and how I was his direct descendent. His story of struggle gave me something to latch onto in difficult times and provided the seeds of an identity as a Greek immigrant descendant. It was his sacrifice that made my life today possible, and I can never allow myself to forget where we came from.

There was a problem in this new-found identity that I had at last found for myself—my immediate family didn't seem to be very "Greek". As far as I could tell, when we were out in public, we didn't seem that different from the other Americans on our block. What happened to some of the more outward cultural traditions and attitudes that made up "Greekness?" We seemed to be missing something. None of my immediate family spoke Greek, not even my grandpa (though he knows a few words). As I got older, it became apparent that things were more complicated than I had at first supposed. It turned out that not everyone in my family was as proud of our Greek heritage as the stories had led me to assume. Through various interactions with family members, I began to piece together a story of stubbornness, fear, and assimilation. It eventually came to light that, although my family managed to preserve something of our Greek heritage, it was in fact Papu, the patriarch of our family, who began the process of assimilation that I observed in the later generations which saddened me as a middle schooler. As it turned out, the dynamic early twentieth century melting pot mentality—as exemplified in Hell's Kitchen—that captivated me as a child had a darker side.

For people like Papu, the difficulties of life in America presented many challenges, particularly regarding the preservation of Greek cultural practices and traditions. Many Greek immigrants abandoned, or at least minimizing their ethnic cultural traditions. This is part of a larger phenomenon of assimilation that I will discuss in greater depth later. In today's world of multicultural expression, many of those challenges have been removed. Therefore, it makes sense to devote new energy towards the examination and propagation of Greek culture. My family's Greek heritage is one example of how this can play itself out today. Even though my parents did not pass down as much to me as they could have, I believe it is possible for me and others to relearn and re-acculturate by studying and reclaiming lost traditions. This can be done by speaking Greek with relatives who represent the culture and learning as much as possible from them. Though I am examining Greek culture in this paper, this idea is certainly transferable to other immigrant cultural contexts.

Although we generally view cultural differences today as interesting aspects of someone's ethnic identity which are to be respected and cherished, many American-born people in Papu's time (early twentieth century) did not appreciate the more unfamiliar cultural aspects of the new Eastern, Southern European, and "Oriental" immigrants that were streaming into cities like New York in the early 1900s. In some parts of America that participated in legislated segregation (such as South Carolina) Greeks were separated from whites in movie theaters and given seating with African-American patrons, so bizarre were they seen in the eyes of Anglo-Americans, who for many years considered Greeks to be

"Oriental" and not necessarily white.[1] People could be so hostile and unaccepting of the less Anglo-American-compatible aspects of Greek and Eastern culture that many Greeks actively chose to mold their public personas around cultural traditions that they perceived to be more "American" or more compatible with "Americanness" to avoid censure and public scrutiny. These individuals chose to suppress their Greek heritage for an American "face" for many reasons, not least of which was to allow their children to assimilate into the American lifestyle that they viewed as superior to the life they left in the home country and to improve job and marriage prospects (Figure 5.1).

For many decades, particularly the 1920s through the 1960s, Greeks in America were actively discouraged by family members and community leaders from looking too "funny" or "Oriental" to the larger American population.[2] Consequently, Greek-Americans of this time were expected to appear publicly in a manner which befit their Anglo-American counterparts. Activities and practices which seemed overly Greek or foreign were discouraged in favor of "American" pursuits. The effects of this unofficial assimilation program were fairly successful. Within two generations, the distinctive national dress and Greek "Oriental" musical styles (such as the *Rebetiko* tradition) were almost completely abandoned while American dress and music were taken up with the rapaciousness and desperation of someone casting off moldy clothes and putting on new ones.[3] Though many movies of the time depict the exploits and struggles of immigrant communities from other countries such as Italy, Greeks and their culture garnered but scant positive attention in the media.

Figure 5.1: Greek immigrants in early twentieth century New York City who acculturated in their dress into American society. Library of Congress Prints and Photographs Division.

By the late 1930s, many Americans were familiar with some of the particulars of Italian and Irish culture and even came to love Italian and Irish delicacies, such as spaghetti (something unknown to Americans until the early twentieth century) and fish-and-chips. These cultural groups also gained negative reputations among the Anglo-American population and gained various nicknames and stereotypes along with these reputations. The Greeks; however, were never afforded that degree of attention. In time, the Greek Orthodox Church in America and the dinner table became the only acceptable places to participate in authentic Greek culture, though these too soon came under threat with increased pressures to assimilate from American Nativists in the 1920s onward. As will be discussed later, starting around the 1940s, even the Church began a process of assimilation during this time, in order to bring itself more in line with Catholicism and Protestantism. Though quite sad, from a current perspective, these changes were felt to be necessary at the time and were considered a matter of self-preservation.

Thus, it is not surprise that Papu decided to try to do everything he could to shed his Greek identity and provide his children with assimilated personas for interacting in American society. To this end, he gave up the Greek music that he had sung in his early youth and took up vigorously the popular songs of American Jazz.[4] He also joined a Free Mason lodge and stopped attending Greek Church (though he returned to it later in life after the death of his wife, which was around the time when I knew him as a toddler), which cut him off from the wider Greek community (though he still kept in contact with his relatives and Greek friends and always did Greek dancing at their weddings).[5] Papu also did everything he could to distance himself from his parents and refused to take trips with them back to Greece in order to avoid looking strange to his American friends.[6] He also made no effort to impart the Greek language to his children, which later prevented my grandfather from joining the Sons of Greece group that met in his town.[7]

Although this may seem bizarre and extreme behavior to us today, at the time, assimilation tendencies were commonplace. Papu was no different from the thousands of other Greek immigrants who decided to do the same circa 1900. I do not resent Papu as I have to acknowledge the difficult situation he was in, which led him to make those decisions. America did not welcome diversity as we know it today and there were many methods for getting immigrants to assimilate. I feel lucky that our Greek background was preserved, though I am grieved by what was lost in transition and translation.

**Literature Review**

Greek American history and preservation needs tilling, since very little research has been done on this immigrant group (and immigrant groups from this region more generally), save by a small number of books by Greek-American authors, (such as Anastasia Christou's *Narratives of Place, Culture and Identity* and George Morrison's *Charleston's Greek Heritage*). While these accounts deal with cultural inheritance, they are generally more geared towards the return Greek immigrant experience in Greece or detailing a particular community's story (generally told from a Western perspective and entirely focused on the parish-church community). Other works may have fewer savory motives such as racially or ethnically assessing Greeks for citizenship-worthiness (as in Henry Pratt Fairchild's *Greek Immigration to the United States*) or for political reasons as in Walter Christmas's *King George of Greece*, which, though an interesting read is more of a history of important Greek political figures. Other than these titles which deal with very specific subtopics, general assessments of the Greek immigrant experience and Greek immigrant cultural heritage and preservation has been little written of.

To fill this gap, I intend to bring to bear the primary sources kept by my family through the use of personal written narratives, interviews (written and oral), photographs, historical documents, and various sundry sources of information to this end. It is my hope that these sources will shed light on the actual conditions experienced by Greeks through the eyes of Papu, By this chapter's conclusion I aim to give the reader valuable insight into the people and attitudes of the times that I intend to study as well as insight into the personal experiences and mentality of Papu. Greek history from the early-mid twentieth century has only been sparsely touched on by scholars in the English language. This era was consumed by Greece becoming involved in a series of wars that greatly impact the people lived there and caused many immigrate to North America. Many of these histories are fairly silent on the experience of life for the average Greek person because of their focus on politicians and military heroes.

Such is the case in Walter Christmas's *King George of Greece*, which, though a very thorough and interesting portrayal of the monarch, was himself a westerner (a Dane, specifically), speaks little to the true condition of the Greek people. In *King George of Greece*, Greek people are generally portrayed as backwards and "other," in sharp contrast to northern European gentry who are often the people writing these accounts. These studies are problematic because of the way they scantly cover the Greek common folk who are portrayed as implacable barbarians in desperate need of European enlightenment. Of course, such treatment does little to provide readers with a genuine sense of Greek culture or of its people. I intend to cover this neglected subject as well as I can through the use of primary documents and materials from my own family and relevant secondary sources that touch on Greek culture.

Concerning the wars experienced by Greece in the twentieth century—I do not have time to give a detailed account of them in this chapter, but the literature about them was nonetheless instrumental in the research I conducted. The relevant secondary literature includes Theodora Dragostinova's "On 'Strategic Frontiers: Debating the Borders of the Post-Second World War Balkans;" Eyal Ginio's *Ottoman Culture of Defeat - the Balkan Wars and Their Aftermath*; and Paul Mojzes's *Balkan Genocides: Holocaust and Ethnic Cleansing in the Twentieth Century,* which mostly deal with geopolitics and the trials, travails, and heady abstract strategies of important statesmen and generals. Mojzes's *Balkan Genocides* does address the experiences of everyday people. These works, though extremely detailed and useful for someone trying to follow the set-piece battles that set the stage for the formation of the political and cultural boundaries of the modern Balkan states, say generally little about the average Greek citizen, much less his or her experience of these tragic events. They are generally written from an early twentieth century western and nationalist perspective, which is fairly unhelpful since Greece's background as an "Oriental" or Eastern country, bolstered by its deep association with the Eastern Orthodox Church lends a different perspective to its people.[8] Still, less is said (or nothing at all) about those Greeks who fled their homeland as refugees, or what life was like for the relatives that they left behind.[9] This is likely because records about them are not in Greece but in the various countries that they fled to, such as the United States.

I drew heavily on relevant content from these books (particularly *Balkan Genocides*) in order to form a picture of the larger events that brought about the conditions that I will be especially concerned with—the plight of Greek immigrant common-folk in America. Though I will certainly draw on the above sources for information related to the large-scale events that effected Greece in the twentieth century. I will bolster these robust sources with primarily material gleaned from my family—especially oral interviews and personal narratives. I will do this in order to tell the stories of the people who actually experienced or fled the events described in these books (such as Papu) with a particular emphasis on what life was like in the abstract as well as how those conditions prompted some Greeks were to leave Greece (Figure 5.2). I will attempt to piece together a coherent narrative account of my individual relatives as well as the story of Greece during the tragic first decades of the twentieth century.

Figure 5.2: Greek immigrants embarking in small boat for steamer for America, Patras, Greece. Library of Congress Prints and Photographs Division.

## Research Methodology

In order to have a more comprehensive grasp on Greek immigrants and their experience in America, as well as the circumstances in Greece during the early-late twentieth century that caused immigration, I have become familiar with a variety of secondary sources. I read extensive sections from secondary sources such as the titles mentioned in the above literature review. I primarily selected books though the College of Charleston Library Database. I used these sources to examine both the biases of and methods used by those studying this subject as well as to accrue general knowledge of life in Greece, but especially the larger political dramas that unfolded there during the era that I am studying. However, in order to better assess conditions experienced by Greek immigrants in the early-mid twentieth century—through the lens of Papu—I was obligated to conduct original research and thus pulled a number of primary sources from a number of places, the method of which I will describe below in the next section. These are primarily things like census records, draft cards, etc.

The primary sources utilized were pulled from Ancestry.com's databanks and from my own personal collection of family documents, photographs, etc. I also used materials from the collections of other family members. I combed through these and selected what was relevant and what was not based on the following criteria: they had to relate to either George Constantine Sigalas (Papu) and/or provide useful information that what was given in oral histories or memoirs from other relatives. A lot of information was unnecessary and therefore excluded if it did not meet the above criteria. I also conducted interviews in order to gather an oral record of my family's Greek history. On the recommendation of certain family members, particularly my uncle, George Constantine Sigalas III, I spoke to two relatives in particular: John Nicholas Patsis and Elias Psylides in order to construct a coherent narrative of events in Greece during the mid- twentieth century as my family experienced it, as well as added tidbits about Papu. These interviews provide the bulk of my material and are the focus of which the rest of the chapter orbits.

I spoke with numerous close family members when interviews with certain relatives were impossible either due to death or temperament. These include my grandfather, George Constantine Sigalas II; my uncle, George Constantine Sigalas III; my aunt, Mary Sigalas; my father, Michael Sigalas; and my mother, Kristin Sigalas. When possible, I also used letters and direct quotations from my ancestors (especially Papu) when they were still alive, when this was impossible. I also collected as much information as possible from interviewees and attempted to gather varying perspectives on the same issue from as many different interviewees as possible. I did this to provide enough ground for further analysis in order to gain a clearer appraisal of the data. Occasionally data provided by the interviews conflicted. When such a seeming conflict of information arose, I attempted to construct a credible narrative by cross-referencing different interviews against each other. Thankfully, this latter method was rarely necessary. I also used primary source documents, which I mentioned in the section on my methodological approach in order to establish facts on a more objective footing, when disagreement was present or when interviewees expressed confusion or uncertainty. Though this situation only occurred with negligible frequency, the results were fruitful.

The combination of secondary and primary sources, as well as the methods that I used to evaluate and analyze them, yielded some interesting results. I was able to validate, by this method, some family stories and legends that had previously appeared to be rather suspect or abstruse. Some of the stories told to me by Papu, or stories that my father told to me about Papu, were examples of the above. I believe that the sorts of sources that I selected as well as the manner and criteria by which I selected them were also fruitful and aided in the construction of accurate examinations of my subject. The secondary sources were useful for generating a general sense of the conditions that my relatives faced in Greece and in inner-city America and they helped to clarify or emphasize many events that my relatives mentioned only in passing or actively downplayed (particularly when said events were highly disturbing to the individuals in question). These sources assisted in forming a picture of the state of prior analysis of this topic as well as the particular emphases that research has put on certain aspects of it as well as any common personal biases that exist within the researching community related to Greek immigration.

The primary sources were particularly helpful because they readily filled in gaps in data that were left by prior research into this topic. Exact details of the lives of my working-class relatives shone through these documents and illuminated many aspects of early twentieth century Greek and Greek-immigrant life not touched upon even cursorily in the existing secondary literature. Filling in this "research gap" is a particular goal of my paper, especially when it covers ground trod by Papu. Through them I was also able to pin down exact dates and locations for events described in secondary sources as well as paint a clear picture of actual real-world examples of the types discussed in secondary literature and in Papu's stories.

Some limitations to my methods—nevertheless—exist. I admit that not every secondary source was examined, and it is entirely possible that some rather important sources may have escaped my notice in part or entirely. This myopia is particularly true in the case of media that only exists in printed form and is not held within the Charleston County Library or the College of Charleston Library. I am limited by my ability to visit archives to collect paper-only sources and so anything which is held outside of the two repositories listed above largely escaped my notice (except when such sources are family documents). I found many of my primary sources by utilizing search functions within the digitized versions of these locations' material both on government websites and through Ancestry.com and these websites have inherent flaws and biases. Though I endeavored to utilize as many search terms as possible in order to glean as many sources as possible from online repositories, certainly some may have escaped my notice.

I also freely admit to an almost total ignorance of the Greek language, particularly in its scholarly written forms, and as such there is much material held in Greece which I am unable to access. Where possible, I utilized Google Translate and other translation programs in order to get some information out of all-Greek sources, but as I lack the ability to successfully navigate all-Greek websites and speak to non-English-speaking Greek relatives in Greece, there is much material that is inaccessible to me. I freely admit that my bias is towards Greece when it comes to many of the international events described in the pages beyond. This bias particularly extends towards the various Greek-Turkish and Greek-Ottoman related conflicts and events that occurred during the twentieth century. This also applies to other significant events in which other nations that antagonized Greece were involved—such as Bulgaria during the Second Balkan War and Germany during World War II. Of course, this bias has limits and does not prevent me from mentioning fault in Greece or the Greek people. I do still retain a preference for and bias towards the Greek side of most conflicts.

I also admit to a decent level of unfamiliarity with many internal aspects of Turkish Islam, which, though the subject only briefly arises within this paper, is still worth bearing in mind. When the topic of Islam in former Ottoman lands does arise, I tend to focus on its relationship to external groups and religions, particularly its relationship with Greek Orthodoxy as well as the Orthodoxies of various Balkan states. I attempt to be upfront about this aspect of my research, unlike some of the sources that I have utilized. Hellenic-bias can be somewhat useful to this scholarship, in a small way, because hardly any secondary sources about the modern Greek state that I could access are written from a Greek perspective, but rather from a Turkish, Serbian, or (former) Yugoslavian perspective. This is especially useful when I deal with immigrant affairs in America, since very little whatsoever is written about Greek immigrants on the whole, especially from a relatively objective internal Greek perspective (other books written by Greeks exist, though these are typically concerned with a niche aspect of Greek immigration, such as race relations or church education while my scope of my research was larger).[10]

While I deal with the larger context of Greek immigration to the United States in the mid-to-late twentieth century, I am primarily interested in the story of my own relatives' immigration and will therefore focus on those experiences. I understand that this method will doubtless fail to include all Hellenic perspectives, but I feel that my relatives are fairly representative of the larger Greek immigrant population, since they span multiple generations and came from mostly very poor classes, though one was perhaps a little better off. While it may be impossible to speak for the entire Hellenic people, it is possible to form a fairly comprehensive view of the experiences and feelings of Greek immigrants—specifically Papu who lived his life, like so many other Greek immigrants, has provided insight into the whole of the Greek immigrant population by virtue of forming a representative sample of such. This forming of a representative sample population was one of the main concepts for my paper that I intended to bring to fruition through the examination of primary source documents related to my family—in this, I have been largely successful. Overall, research on my relatives has yielded few insights both into myself and into the circumstances of Greeks who came to America in the twentieth century—specifically Papu.

**Part A: One Family's Passage**

My surname, Sigalas, has an interesting origin. According to family oral history, our last name originated on the island of Santorini in the Greek Aegean, near Crete. Some of this interesting background was preserved by Papu, when he mentioned that in his parent's hometown that practically everyone had the name Sigalas. He used to tell us, "It was like being named Smith here in America... that's what everyone was called... it's a very common name there."[11] My uncle, who had the opportunity to visit Santorini in 2017, confirmed Papu's stories.[12] According to him, many businesses and restaurants on that picturesque island are still run by people who bear our name, some of whom are our relatives. In the early 1890s, Papu, moved to Athens and married an orphaned girl named Marie. There isn't much information about her, but according to family lore, at some point she worked for the Royal Family of Greece as a nursemaid.[13]

With the coming of the Second Balkan War (1912-1913) facilitated by the assassination of King George I of Greece by an anarchist radical in the summer of 1912, the Sigalas family left Greece that autumn from Pireaus, aboard the ship *Patris* for America.[14] About a month later, they landed at Ellis Island. According to my great grandfather, his family (like so many immigrants during that time) were kept in "cage-like cells" and were interrogated to reveal whether they were anarchists or spies.[15] After a thorough and humiliating medical examination and quarantine period, they were later discharged and eventually leased an apartment in a tenement at 265 West Fortieth Street in Hell's Kitchen, Manhattan.[16] Their apartment was a "cold water flat" which meant that it was small and had no heat, hot running water, or toilets in the entire building, all of which were by that time features in most homes.[17]

Their adopted neighborhood, Hell's Kitchen, was a notoriously dangerous and shoddy place composed almost entirely of large blocks of tenement apartments that provided only the basic rudiments of shelter necessary to survive.[18] Though wealthy New Yorkers began housing reform initiatives in the late 1890s to alleviate conditions in tenements, life in Hell's Kitchen was miserable and most families had either no windows or no ventilation and frequently neither. With thousands of people crammed into small and unsafe apartments, disease epidemics and fires were frequent. Many deaths often went unreported either because no one cared or due to pressure from landlords, eager to prevent a crackdown and loss of profits. Papu's own building was 1,000 feet long and four stories high and 5,000 to 9,000 people lived there (only about a dozen of which were Greek).[19] During the early 1900s Hell's Kitchen was a refuge for "undesirable immigrants." Though it was originally founded by Irish, by the time Papu lived there it had gained a large contingent of Italians and other disaffected groups from various areas in Europe.[20] Already, we can see the crucible into which Greek immigrants were being poured. Maintaining a strong cultural identity in "Hellish" conditions, such as existed in Hell's Kitchen, was difficult.

**Part B: A Look at Tenement "Alley Culture"**

In the early twentieth century, Hell's Kitchen was considered to be the most dangerous neighborhood in America, rampant with crime, especially theft and murder.[21] Hell's Kitchen was so dangerous that the New York Police Department (mostly staffed by Irish at this time) refused to patrol the area except in large groups. Even then, "cop sniping"—the practice of throwing refuse or bricks at passing policemen was a pastime.[22] In many ways, it was a lawless place where everyone was divided into clans and tight-knit extended family units.[23]

This environment created the ideal conditions for the formation of fully-organized gangs. These gangs, originally founded by Irish, Italians, and other groups in the early 1900s, were at first loose collections of local tough guys who banded together to survive.[24]

Starting in the 1910s, some of these gangs crystalized into early organized crime groups. Some of the gangs Papu personally encountered or knew of were the Gophers (an early powerful Irish gang), La Cosa Nostra (the Sicilian crime syndicate that later became the Mafia) and the Camorra (an Italian organization that competed with the Mafia early on), the Gas House Gang, Murder Incorporated (actual name), the Chicago Outfit (which had influence there and occasionally sent out hitmen), and even the Jewish Mafia (primarily Dutch Schultz's outfit). These gangs were in near constant conflict with each other and violent clashes in the streets were frequent, leaving many grieving families and civilian casualties. As such, Papu's memoirs are filled with references to these and other gangs and he witnessed much violence in his early life, loosing many friends and acquaintances to gang violence.[25] Though he was never a part of a gang, these thugs were a constant threat to people like Papu and his friends. Daily life for the average poor immigrant in Hell's Kitchen was a frightening, complex, high-stakes and ever-changing dance of gang politics. This environment caused Papu to be bitter and he eventually sought a safer and calmer life. Understandably, this sort of frightening environment caused many to associate Hell's Kitchen with their ethnic background which consequently led many to attempt to leave both behind, like Papu.

In those days, everyone in Hell's Kitchen was forced to pay bribes (so-called "protection money") to whichever gang controlled the territory you worked in. Those who refused to pay or protested in any way were often found weeks later dead in the sewers or on their own doorstep with a hole in their chest or a knife in their back.[26] Papu's old stories indicate that it wasn't always safe for immigrants, even if they did pay the protection money the gangs asked for. Sometimes, rival gangs would see payment to another as an insult due to some perceived right to control your block and would knife you for that anyway—or at least beat you until you were black-and-blue. This situation was complicated by the preponderance of what Papu called "tough guys," who were gang-affiliated or crime-adjacent but who more or less acted as free-agent "bullies." These men, generally called "thugs" or "hoods," used their self-proclaimed street connections to extort money from vulnerable people to line their own pockets.

Since "oriental" immigrants tended to fare poorly in the legal system and were infrequently protected by police, people like my Papu were especially vulnerable. Some of these thugs were more air than muscle and it could sometimes be difficult to tell whether you were talking to Al Capone or Dutch Schultz's right-hand-man or to some wannabe. You had to have highly-adapted street knowledge of a given neighborhood and its people. Some free-lance thugs were essentially bluffing and could be beaten off with little-to-no repercussions. Others could hardly be spat at without the night ending with you and your family's bodies floating down the Hudson River. Thus, an immigrant like Papu had to think smart if he wanted to survive the reality of life in gang-controlled Hell's Kitchen.

Papu saw all of this growing up and, in my opinion, it molded him into a tough-as-nails, extremely stubborn, and bitter man. He stood up for himself when encountered by the largely English-speaking hoodlums who threatened him, but this led to difficulties later in life. This sort of no-nonsense attitude made it easy for him to get into conflict with his relatives much more easily than most. A particularly good example of Papu's unwillingness to bend under extremely threatening circumstances is recorded in his ad-hoc memoirs, which are provided. I took the liberty of adding titles to the following narrative in order to better organize them.

**Part C: Memories of Violence**
**The First Two Dollar Fight**

*There were two $2 fights. The one I'd rather talk about happened a couple of years before the second. It was with some character from Skillman Street: about 5'10", 170–180lbs. I was 5'6", and I weighed 126lbs (until I got married).*

*He talked like a tough guy—in gangster ways if you ever watched some old movies. He asked how much I would charge to change the rear bearing on his Packard car. I answered $2. That was some job. I had no press, but $2 in 1932 was money. He had the bearing. He got it from the junkie a couple of blocks from the shop.*

*I told him right then that if that bearing didn't fit, it would cost the $2 labor, and he ordered me, "Do it!"*

*So I had a heck of a job getting the old bearing off with a hammer and chisel, and I tried not to break it just in case I had to put it back on.*

*I got it off, and the bearing he had was wrong—too loose. I asked him to go to the junkie and get the right one or go across the street to the parts store and get a new one.*

*He said, like a tough guy, "Put the old back on."*

*I told him right then that he would still have to pay me the $2.*

*He repeated, "Put it back on."*

*I said, "Okay, but you're going to pay."*

*He pointed at the axle and said, "Do it."*

*So I put it on and installed the axle.*

*He got in his touring car and started backing toward the door. I rushed and closed the doors. He said he would go through them.*

*I said, "You have a license plate, and I have a good memory, so do what you want to do."*

*He said, "I guess I'll have to take care of you," and opened the door to come out. Before the door opened all the way, I reached and grabbed him by whatever he was wearing around his neck—maybe a tie.*

*I said, "Let me help you out," and half-pulled him out.*

*As he was ready to come out, he turned white from fright, and proved to be like all the bullies that I ever came across.*

*He said, "Okay. Here's your $2."*

*I didn't get a tip. I guess I lost a customer.*

**The Second Two Dollar Fight**

*The second $2 fight was forced on me, and I was stubbornly stupid. It was January 1933. I was 25 years old. It was the second Sunday after New Year's, and [I was] celebrating something at John's (Pearl's brother's) house. I went to a beer joint to get a gallon of wine. It was illegal, but some Italian there knew another [sic] that made some at home.*

*Most of the people there were Italians, but only about 5-percent of the young ones thought they were tough guys. They knew—or at least tried to impress you by naming—Joe Bonono— "Joe Bananas," they called him. He went state's evidence against some of the Mob about five years ago. I believe it was in the papers.*

*Also, there was a Joe Farmer who made his bootleg beer in the basement of Mr. Tony Angeloni, [where there was a] U.S. Marshall office, on the first floor. The second floor was the speakeasy.*

*I worked at 839 Bedford Avenue; the speakeasy was two doors away.*

*[The wine] cost $2.50. I gave the guy a $5 bill, and he came back with the gallon and my change. Looking around, I had noticed some sleazy characters, so I didn't*

*want to open my wallet; I put the $2.50 in my vest pocket and I was asked by the fellow about the empty gallon I had bought the week before.*

*I told him, "Come with me, and I'll get it." I went out and sat in my car—a 1927 Chevrolet—and waited a few minutes. My doors opened and one guy on my left stuck the point of a knife on the back of my neck and asked me for my wallet.*

*It wasn't funny. I had to think fast. I told them that there would be a lot of commotion before that knife worked, and that I came from Hell's Kitchen, and if they knew Andy Gavern and Salty (they weren't friends of mine, but I knew of them), and that we from Hell's Kitchen did what they were doing, different.*

*Well, I guess I impressed them. They put the knife away, and I threw a lot of B.S. Finally, they said, "Just give us the $2 you put in your pocket."*

*Before that, I told the guy on my left to close the door, since it was cold, so he went back to continue our talk.*

*Suddenly, the fellow on my right nodded. The fellow behind me got a chokehold on me. The guy on my right swung at me and missed. I swung at him and missed because the guy behind had pulled my head back. I got my right foot up, I remember being careful not to kick the gallon of wine, and I got him on the chest and kicked him. I then put my feet on the overhead. My one foot slipped and went through the windshield. Somehow, I managed to get both feet at the top, and went back over the seat and broke this guy's grip, and as I landed, I punched him as he opened the door to run at the same time as I punched this guy, the other guy was coming in the other door and I tried to kick him, but he saw his buddy run out, he done the same.*

*They didn't get the $2[.50], but I broke a windshield—$300 from a junkyard—and I had to repair all the hinge posts. They were made of wood in those days, and the top hinge was completely off, and the bottom was just barely* *holding. Most of my bottom teeth got chipped when I squeezed between the top of the seat with his forearm on my throat.*

*Someone called Johnny Tarzen, the cop on the beat, and a friend of mine. Johnny asked me, "Could you point them out if you saw them?" He said that if I could, he would lock them up.*

*Well, that area had a friend who knew some gangsters from South Brooklyn who were part of Al Capone's gang, and I was operating a shop around the corner from there. If I pressed charges, I might lose some customers, besides running the chance of retaliation. I told Johnny all I wanted was to be put in a cell with each one of them and nobody would bother me anymore. The cop declined. So much for that.*

Obviously, this is a harrowing story. As a child, I had no frame of reference for the kind of violence described by Papu in his narrative. Indeed, when I was in my preteen years, I tended to think that these stories were interesting, exciting even. I used to think that the kind of experiences described by Papu, of life in the tenements, fights, brush-ups with the police, etc., sounded "fun." To a boyish mind, having to punch and kick your way out of a mugging by armed mafia-connected assailants in your own car seemed like a good time. Riding around the city in semi-stolen cars sounded exciting too, I did not understand the implications of these things. I grew up in lower-class late twentieth century suburban neighborhoods. This kind of densely populated, dangerous, and gritty urban life, as found in Hell's Kitchen, made a huge impression on me, but for the wrong reasons. Instead of seeing the kind of rough inner-city life that people like Papu lived in as a tragic episode in American urban history, I saw it as a sort of silver-screen silent urban drama like Charlie Chaplin's *The Kid* (which was heavily recommended by Papu) or an exciting private eye *noir* story, like Raymond Chandler's *Phillip Marlow* radio series (which I enjoyed as a child). In these fictional depictions of life in hellish tenement neighborhoods, the shady and unscrupulous villains always lost and the plucky tenement-raised heroes with hearts of gold always came out on top and never got seriously hurt, physically or mentally.

Sometimes, like in *The Kid*, the wealthy descend into the tenements to raise up the protagonist to their Olympian realm. The reality was this era of American urban history was dirty, dangerous, cramped, and oppressive. The reason Papu was around to tell my grandfather, father, and I about his exciting back-street brawls was precisely *because he left* Hell's Kitchen. Its only fun and exciting as a listener to these stories, and not as someone who had to live through it, or worse-yet, someone who was killed by it. Papu did not want to stay in a place where he felt inferior and under frequent threats of violence. Another story he used to tell illustrates my point.

**The Gas House Gang Encounter**

*Here's one. When I relate this to anyone, I feel they believe I'm exaggerating. Eddy had an Essex car, and I don't recall how he was taking me to work. I lived on 103rd Street at the time, and he offered to take me to work. He had another guy named Frank and his girlfriend in the back, and I got in the back with them as there was another fellow, Ray, sitting with Eddy.*

*Well, he got down between Twelfth and Eleventh Street on Third Avenue, which had elevated trains above, and naturally, steel structures supporting the tracks above. (These don't exist anymore; they were sold as scrap to Japan.)*

*This was about 1930. Some Buick made a U-turn in front of Eddy, kind of slow, and Eddy yelled out, jokingly, "Get that load out of the way!"*

*The guy in the Buick said, "What?"*

*Eddy said, "You heard what."*

*The guy made another U-turn and stopped behind us. The driver got out of his car, as did Eddy.*

*Eddy walked up to the guy. I don't know who threw the first punch or took the first swing, but when I looked back from the window, the guy was sprawled on the fender, and his companion got out from the other side to get at Eddy.*

*Ray, seeing this, got out to get the second guy. Then I noticed a couple of guys coming from across the street, from another Buick. These guys were not young men in their early twenties—they were men about 35 or better, wearing Fedora hats, and looked like typical gangsters you see in old movies. They went over to beat on Eddy and Ray.*

*I got out. Another Buick stopped behind the other one. Some more guys got out. I don't know how many, but we were getting mobbed.*

*Well, I done the smart thing, separating guys wherever I could, saying it wasn't a fair fight, and somehow, I had some influence. I think at least I wasn't getting hit.*

*Suddenly, out of the butcher shop, where all the fighting was taking place, a pudgy little Irishman, 5'7", 180lbs, came out with a meat cleaver in his hand.*

*I didn't know what he was going to do.*

*He asked, with a good Irish brogue, "Is it a fight?" And then added, "By Christ, it is!" He wrapped his cleaver in his butcher's apron and threw it back into the store—I can still see it sliding on the sawdust.*

*Well, he started swinging haymakers at anyone standing, and because my guys were busy sometimes down on top of others, and this guy didn't care, he was going to beat everybody.*

*Well, finally I saw Ray bleeding from under his eye—and one of the gangsters wearing brass knuckles. I saw my job: I pulled Eddy from—I don't remember—on top of a guy, or pulled the guy from Eddy, and yelled to Ray and Eddy both to run for it.*

*I ran and got into the Essex. Eddy got in the other way, and I stuck in gear and started moving.*

*Ray was running alongside, looking for a chance to jump in, but as the elevated train* [i.e. EL] *were there, it was difficult. The door on the Essex opened outward from the doorpost, making it impossible to close, swinging back toward the rear.*

*Well, I got it close to an EL pillar, and hit the pillar with the door. It broke the strap and the door swung back, and I slowed down for Ray to jump in.*

*Just then, a Buick—again, maybe one of three or four Buicks—cut me off. I couldn't do anything because there were pushcarts on the right side of the EL pillars.*

*A guy, I'll never forget him—he was about 35—came over, opened the door and said, "Oh, you were with them! Come out and get yours."*

*I told him, "Stand back, and give me a chance to get out."*

*A cop came over, God bless him, and asked this guy, in a good Irish brogue, "And what are you about to do to this fellow?" (meaning me.)*

*The fellow said, "Oh, nothing. We had an argument."*

*The cop said to him, "Argument me ass. I saw the whole thing. You guys mobbed them."*

*I really don't know how much he saw; actually, from the butcher shop to the corner was about 100 feet or so, and as much as took place, I don't think it lasted more than three to five minutes.*

*But anyway, he asked me what I was doing there, and I told him I was on my way to work.*

*He told the other guy, "Get back to Eleventh Street where you belong," and told me to get going.*

*In the meantime, Ray kept running. As he explained a few days later when I saw him, when Ray saw that I was stopped, he ran up Eleventh Street where there was a little Italian restaurant frequented by the elite when they went slumming. He ran through the restaurant, grabbed a folded napkin from a table occupied by some people, and ran through the kitchen, where the cook looked at him, wondering what was going on with a guy running through a kitchen, holding a napkin over his bleeding eye.*

*Ray ran out the back door, jumped a fence (he told me he thought someone was behind him), and went to a small local hospital—I don't remember the name, I think "Doctor's Hospital." He had his eye taken care of, and that finishes the story of how we got mobbed by the Gas House Gang, another area like Hell's Kitchen.*

**Ally Hall's Death**

*Ally Hall was about the same age as Eddy and Carly—I guess 18 or 19. He heard the Gas House Gang story and he wanted to go with us back down there and see if we could get into a fight and have them chase us up to the 103rd Street Dance Hall, so we could run up there and get all the guys up there involved.*

*I thought it would be funny; I liked the idea of getting even, but never would have gone through with it—especially after Ally said he had a gun.*

*Eddy, as well as I, would have no part of it. Ally was the type that always got in fights as long as Eddy was around, as I later found from Carlo.*

*I didn't like him. He used to steal my car for joy rides, and I used to report it stolen to the police, because I was of a different character—especially with him having a gun. But when I caught him, I warned him that if he ever got near my car, I was going to kick the ***** out of him, and he quit.*

*He was yellow; that's why the gun.*

*Well, it wasn't much later, Ally was found dead on the stoop of his apartment house. I guess he had a fractured skull.*

The last sentence is particularly interesting: the detail of his erstwhile friend's murder is related so matter-of-factly that it passed right by me as a child. I never noticed the fact that this, like so many of Papu's stories, is a tale of violence and the injustice and terrible pain inflicted of a world ruled by fists, brass knuckles, broken bottles, knives, and guns. My great grandfather grew up in terrible slums and was merely trying to get by while avoiding being a target of "bullies" and dangerous gangsters. These were men who killed without pity or fear until they were imprisoned or killed, and Papu knew this. Prohibition in Hell's Kitchen, though doubtless exciting, was not a great time to live through and involved a lot of suffering. People like Papu did not get the option to grow up to be respectable, docile citizens—they had to fight tooth and nail just to survive the beatdown that life threw at them. In neighborhoods like Hell's Kitchen, back then, most people did not solve things diplomatically and had no interest in doing so—every small dispute was solved violently. Some of this violence is shocking to me now that I understand the implications of it. It's shocking how quickly simple arguments escalated to full-blown fisticuffs or even outright murder, as was illustrated in the above story.

The following three stories illustrate this point. They are unique also, among the narratives that I have chosen to include in that they are quite short. I would argue that this brevity and matter-of-fact-ness is indicative of a man and a culture that had become completely desensitized to senseless violence. Unlike the previous narratives, Papu does not bother giving the specific details of the fight, he simply reported that there was one and that it can be seen in the narratives what the outcome was.

## Eddy Didn't Back Down

*I'm happy to say I met Carlo (Sylvio Carly) somehow on 103rd Street, where I lived. He told me how Eddy, his friend, had stolen a late-model Studebaker sometime back, I guess—when he was about 16, and both of them used to ride around just for fun. Eddy took personal care of the car; the rugs and upholstery had to be clean, just like it was his. It must have been a deluxe model, as it had small flower vases in the back by the side windows.*

*Carlo was a nice fellow, and I finally met Eddy. He was known to get into fights and never back down, and he was good with his fists—never knives, guns, bats, bottles. He was my kind of guy.*

*The only problem was that he would do anything not to back down, even with the police. One cop hit him with a club across his feet because he had fallen asleep on an empty banana stand. Eddy got up and punched the cop in the mouth and knocked out some teeth.*

*A second cop came on the scene. They called a cab, and both of them forced Eddy into the cab, and while one was holding Eddy, the other hit Eddy across the mouth with his club and broke all his front teeth.*

*Eddy wasn't arrested. The cops knew they were wrong, and it was a personal grudge. This happened just before I met him.*

## An Aborted Knife Fight

*I had another experience on 9th Avenue in Hell's Kitchen. Six Latinos came into a restaurant and wanted to beat up this little Greek. I stopped it, but one [of them] challenged me, so I went out [outside with him]. One of the customers came out, and as I called this guy to [fight] me, the customer warned me that he had a knife.*

*I threw my hands up, and both of us quit. You never know what you're getting into.*

**The Deaths of Eddie Courtney and Artie Huttick**

*Then there were two friends of mine, Eddie Courtney and Artie Huttick. Eddie was a fine fellow but wouldn't back down to anything.*

*Artie Huttick was a light heavyweight boxing champion of 1930. He got stabbed to death by two sailors. He tried to help a young girl who was being abused by the sailors.*

*He had just started fighting pro [again].*

Some notes on the above story: Arthur Huttick, (1910-1937) was the 1930 National Golden Gloves light-heavyweight boxing champion, according to newspapers, and was murdered on November 8, 1937, on a side street in Manhattan. Huttick had helped reveal a fight-throwing ring in February 1937, and many speculated that his murder was either in retribution or as a way of silencing him—perhaps something else was brewing like another fight ring. From the available records, however, it appears that he had not fought professionally since 1934. Papu meant that he was just starting to restart his career after the drama surrounding the scandal.[27]

**Part D: Preservation Angle**

Now that we have received these stories and seen how they represent incredible suffering and struggle—we are led to ask the question: What remains of this crazy world of gangsters and their dirty alleyways today? Is all of this simply a setting for crime-thrillers in Hollywood movies and no longer something that actually exists in the world as a monument to the people who used to live there? Though some research has been done on tenement culture, (which is obviously the main thrust of Papu's narratives) that research tends to focus on the social and economic reasons for the development of the urban underclass, and how to address it. For many years, arguably right up until the 1980s, rough-and-tumble urban immigrant culture was seen as a kind of blight on cities—something that made them unsafe and unattractive to white middle class Americans.[28] Only recently have serious energies been expended on the preservation of this once-despised culture and its physical testaments. Such examples can be seen in projects such as the New York Tenement Museum in the Lower East Side, in a select few books, and various blogs scattered throughout the internet.[29]

Little of this once vibrant historic urban fabric remains in America's cities today, largely because it was either thought to be of little value or because cities were actively trying to remove tenements and similar dense urban configurations.[30] Of the four tenement apartment buildings that Papu and his family lived in between 1912 and 1925, none survive.[31] This is tragic when one considers the sheer number of people who once lived in those buildings or in whose shadow life played itself out. These tenements and associated neighborhoods were unique in America's history. New York's immigrant communities inhabited tenement neighborhoods, particularly Hell's Kitchen, which were considered among the most dangerous places to live in the country but were also home to some of America's most underrepresented groups, such as Greek immigrants.

Across America, once vibrant and diverse, densely packed urban communities have disappeared over the last six decades, flattened by what people used to call progress, primarily through the drastic "slum clearing" interventions of Robert Moses and his contemporaries in the twentieth century.[32] Few of these original slum neighborhoods (or even individual buildings that composed them) survive and, I would argue, very little of the original vibrancy has continued into the present day. This is especially true when one considers the curious mixture of backgrounds that used to occur. In cities like New York today, there may be a Little Italy (though typically few Italians remain), or a Little Puerto Rico, or China Town, but few of these places are the real "melting pots" of Papu's time. Smaller immigrant community groups, like Greeks, have been able to preserve as much of their ancestral culture in the places in which they live or lived.

Hell's Kitchen was once America's worst neighborhood, a place that police only visited in force. Unbelievably, is now a place for wealthy Anglo-Americans to buy fancy condominiums in brand-new high-rises that do nothing to reference or respect the struggle that immigrant communities like the Greeks had to face. One of the addresses that Papu mentioned was 265 West 40th Street, which was bulldozed. By 1929 the site had a large and imposing Art Deco style "loft building." In 2009, the location was bulldozed again and replaced with a completely soulless, extremely modern glass building which now houses a Muji Brand Clothing retail store. [33] Gone are the interesting byways and winding alleyways of the past. These places have been totally and rapidly "redeveloped" with little regard for the memories and ancestors that used to inhabit them.

While this is by no means a unique story in contemporary American urban experience, (re)development like this is especially detrimental for Greeks since these former melting pot neighborhoods were the loci of late nineteenth and early twentieth century ethnic communities. For example, with some minor exceptions, the Greek café, so long a staple and stereotypical feature of Greek community life, has disappeared. Greek Orthodox congregations have relocated to the suburbs of their respective urban areas. These changes have done nothing to improve the integrity of the urban Greek ethnic immigrant identity, since they have in part led to a large-scale trend among Greeks towards suburban acculturation. Suburbanization proves to be the death of any real traditional culture, especially a communal social system like the Greek one because it becomes fractured and disjointed. Greek Americans must work hard to maintain an ethnic identity. Greek parents often wonder if their children will acculturate. Without major changes in the American social mores and fabric, it is difficult to foresee any real level of improvement on this front.

**Part E: Greek Cultural Traditions and Practices in America and at Home**

So, what are my Greek cultural practices and traditions and why should they be preserved? Greece, a small country at the crossroads of European, Eurasian, and Eastern Mediterranean (or Oriental) civilization, has a unique culture. When Greeks came to the United States in the twentieth century, they initially came with cultural legacy and baggage that their ethnicity entailed. Gradually, some assimilated into American society. Of course, people do not lose their culture overnight and for no reason. It must be acknowledged that the pressures for Greeks, such as Papu to adopt the outward expressions of American culture were very strong. It was because of these assimilation pressures to assimilate that much cultural practice was lost in some families or only preserved in rump form. These sorts of cultural practices are broad in scope, and they include: the Greek Orthodox religion and associated rituals, such as folk music (like Rebetiko), traditional dance, Eastern Mediterranean foodways, clothing, among others.[34]

**Part G: The Greek Orthodox Church**

Of all the cultural practices brought to America by Greeks like Papu, Greek Orthodox Christianity is clearly the most important, not only from a religious perspective but also from a social one. This is also the best-preserved of imported Greek traditions. Notable Greek Orthodox traditions that were brought over by immigrants of this faith, with its rich architectural legacy, liturgical practices, and sacred music. It has been said of the Greek relationship to Greek Orthodoxy that: "…to the form of his religion, the Greek is decidedly loyal. A Greek is born to his religion just as he is to his nationality… it forms an important part of the constitution of every Greek community."[35] Since Greek culture has grown and adapted along the contours of Orthodoxy, it is impossible to describe Greek culture without also including this aspect of Christianity. From birth, nearly every ethnic Greek is a part of the life of the Church. The baby is born into the world after a period of intense prayer by the whole community and, forty days later after the mother is declared ritually clean again. The baby is baptized into the Church and thus the child is made a participant in Christ's body. The baby is then given a baptismal cross, which they will wear for the rest of their life. This cross is often blessed by the matriarch of the family to ward off the all-feared *vaskania* or *mati*—the Evil Eye, though this is not strictly an Orthodox practice. The child then grows up hearing the beautiful Byzantine chant of the Church's choir and cantor. Boys can also become an acolyte (or altar-server), and so on until adulthood.[36]

Important holidays and rites include Holy Lent, Holy *Pascha* (our most sacred and celebrated holiday), participating in *Theophany,* braiding palm fronds for Palm Sunday, leaving food and candles at the tombs of family members, and participated in the annual Twelve Great Feasts of the Paschal cycle. For marriage, the bride receives a crown, rings, and candles, and the groom participates in his own rituals. Lamb is also slaughtered, for a great feast. Some Greek men become monks (the crucible of Orthodox life and culture), where they progress through successive tonsuring until he becomes a *raso* monk, eventually becoming a monk of the *megaloschema*. The entire year is punctuated by various days of sacred significance.

All of what I have described here takes place in Greece and in America with great regularity. The general format of services and traditions have survived the transatlantic voyage as well as the passage of time. The Greek Orthodox Church, as practiced in America, sadly has faltered due to intense external pressures to assimilate, making it difficult in some ways to preserve authentic Greek religious traditions. This was mostly due to the Westernizing effects of acculturation and assimilation had on Greek immigrants, especially their children. Similar to how Papu did not pass along certain Greek cultural traditions because of the intense pressures of "melting pot" ideology and straight-out prejudice leveled against people like him by non-Greeks, many succumbed to similar pressures and felt forced to "adapt" into something more American.

Though the Greek Orthodox Church in America generally follows the same format as all other Orthodox churches, there are some stark differences. Generally, all Greek Orthodox churches are oriented towards the east and contain a *narthex* (or entrance hall), a *naos* (or main sanctuary), side aisles, *anastasis*, apse, *iconostasis* (icon screen), altar, *cathedra* (throne), as well as other distinct features. While American Greek Orthodox parish churches follow this format, many also contain pews and pipe organs, which are foreign to traditional Orthodox church design. These additions, so unique to Greek Orthodox American parishes are virtually unheard of in Greece and other countries where Orthodoxy is present. This is largely the result of twentieth century Greek immigrants acculturating to Protestant American standards of worship. These changes were made to soften the "strangeness" of their "Oriental" religion at a time when religious tolerance was not necessarily a high priority for many Americans. During these decades even Catholicism was viewed with suspicion by Protestant America, especially considering the recorded instances of violent attacks against Catholic parishes by Protestant rioters during these times.[37]

Greeks living in America were faced with a bigger dilemma than were their Irish, Italian, and Polish Catholic immigrant counterparts, since Greek Orthodox Christianity was considered even more stranger to Protestant Americans.[38] Consequently, there was a great push in the mid-1900s (though it began in the 1920s) to conform the Orthodox Church to Protestant American expectations.[39] This occurred in myriad ways, aside from the aforementioned pews and pipe organs. Many Greek Orthodox churches, for example, were generically named things like Holy Trinity Orthodox Christian Church, in order to clearly identify them as both Christian (which is of course a redundant thing to say, since it comes right after "Orthodox" and "Trinity"), Trinitarian (which is very important for Protestants, since it is the rubric by which they typically evaluate whether they consider a sect to be properly Christian or a heresy), and that it is a "Church," which again, is redundant. They made efforts to ensure the external "Americanness" of their religion. For example, starting in the 1940s, Orthodox clerics adopted Western clerical garments when in public so that they would not seem "weird" to American observers.[40] Of course, this stands in contrast to traditional Greek Orthodox practices regarding what garments priests should wear, but such was the intense fear held by many Orthodox of their inability to "fit in" with American society. In my opinion, I find these alterations to be unfortunate, though I acknowledge that they may have been necessary at the time.

The desire to fit in is understandable, even today. Allow me to relate a story I heard about a Greek

Orthodox hermit in Appalachia: a nun was sent to begin a hermitage in a mountainous region of Tennessee. The people she interacted with there were so confused by this female monk (attired as she was in long black robes and fez-like skullcap and veil) that the locals thought she was a pious Muslim and refused her service at restaurants and even some stores. The poor woman had to petition her bishop to allow her to stitch a cross into her *skufia* so that people would let her buy things. If things like this happen in today's world of highspeed internet and cable news, one can only imagine the sorts of prejudice that Greeks had to face previously.

**Conclusion**

Many might not understand the importance of researching and remembering the stories of their family' past. However, if there is one thing that history has taught us, it is that it tends to repeat itself. Though the 1920s are long gone, the 2020s are still very much present, the Greeks, Italians, Jews, Poles, and other ethnic groups of the early twentieth century have been replaced by new "others". In today's United States, Latinx have taken on the mantle of the marginalized immigrant out-group. Each day, thousands of Latinx immigrants' stream into this country, not unlike the Greeks of a century ago. Locked within dangerous neighborhoods, unable to move into larger society because of language barriers, in-group politics, and prejudice, these new immigrants face similar challenges to the Greeks of Papu's day. If we allow ourselves to learn from the people of Papu's generation through their histories and their stories, perhaps we would be better able to deal with issues such as the ones Latinx immigrants are facing presently. This is part of what makes preservation so important—it allows us to take a peek into the past and learn something valuable about why a place or cultural tradition matters. By understanding why something from the past matters, we can better plan for how our important places and should be for the future, thus making it an inheritance that we can give to our children (Figure 5.3).

Humanity is essentially the same today as it was one hundred or even one thousand years ago. Therefore, would it not be wiser to see the struggles of our ancestor's pasts as something akin to the suffering of people from the present time, who are also experiencing a similar calamity? Immigrants and refugees are still people –still human beings! If we allow ourselves and our society to forget what was done wrong in the past, *we* risk repeating the horrors that our own ancestors experienced. This would completely efface their memory of what they did for us to thrive in the present, through our gross negligence regarding what our inheritance cost them to have. Can we not do better than this? Can we not pull our ancestors from out of the mire of oblivion and save them from drowning in obscurity by treating contemporary immigrants and refugees better than our ancestors were treated? Our immigrant ancestors would have wanted to be treated with dignity and allowed to live in peace. We don't have to exclude people from our communities just because they have customs that are different from our own. We have the chance to make right past mistakes by others, now. It is up to us to live as better people and learn from the past for a better future.

Figure 5.3: Greek American children at a Hellenic Festival, Buffalo, New York, 1982. Photograph by Lydia M. Fish. Retrieved from the Library of Congress, https://www.loc.gov/item/afc1993001_197823_04/.

## Additional Readings

The following are additional readings on *What is Your Heritage and the State of its Preservation?*

Barry L. Stiefel, ed. *What is Your Heritage and the State of its Preservation?, Volume IV: Our Roots Run Deep* (Berwyn Heights, MD: Heritage Books, Inc. 2021).

Barry L. Stiefel, ed. *What is Your Heritage and the State of its Preservation?, Volume III: Putting Theory into Practice* (Berwyn Heights, MD: Heritage Books, Inc., 2018).

Barry L. Stiefel, ed. *What is Your Heritage and the State of its Preservation?, Volume II: Collaborations with Storyboard America* (Berwyn Heights, MD: Heritage Books, Inc. 2016).

Barry L. Stiefel, ed. *What is Your Heritage and the State of its Preservation?: Essays on Family History Exploration from the Field* (Berwyn Heights, MD: Heritage Books, Inc., 2014).

Barry L. Stiefel, "'The Places My Granddad Built': Using Popular Interest in Genealogy as a Pedagogical Segue to Historic Preservation", in *Human-Centered Built Environment Heritage Preservation: Theory and Evidence-Based Practice*, edited by Barry L. Stiefel and Jeremy C. Wells. New York: Routledge, 2018), 289-308.

Barry L. Stiefel, "Beyond Names and Dates on a Tree: How Librarians Can Help Explore Family Heritage and Preservation", in *Librarianship and Genealogy: Trends, Issues, Case Studies*, Carol Smallwood, ed. (Jefferson, NC: McFarland & Company, 2018), 156-63.

# Endnotes for What is Your Heritage and the State of its Preservation?, Volume 5: Connections to Place

---

**Endnotes for Introduction**

[1] Barry L. Stiefel, ed. *What is Your Heritage and the State of its Preservation?, Volume 4: Our Roots Run Deep* (Berwyn Heights, MD: Heritage Books, Inc., 2020).

**Endnotes Chapter 1**

[1] Simon J. Bronner, "Shenandoah Valley Region," in *Encyclopedia of American Folklife* (Armonk, NY: M.E. Sharpe, 2006), 1118-1120.
[2] U.S. Census Bureau 2020. 2020 Decennial Census. Retrieved from https://data.census.gov/cedsci/all?q=Sylvester%20town,%20West%20Virginia.
[3] Bronner, *Encyclopaedia of American Folklife*, 1118-1120.
[4] Bronner, *Encyclopedia of American Folklife*, 1118-1120.
[5] Department of Historic Resources, "007-0700 Lewis Shuey House," Virginia Department of Resources (The Commonwealth of Virginia, 2020), https://www.dhr.virginia.gov/historic-registers/007-0700/.
[6] Bronner, *Encyclopedia of American Folklife*, 1118-1120.
[7] Althea Webb, "African Americans in Appalachia," Oxford African American Studies Center, 1 March 2013, https://oxfordaasc.com/page/featured-essay-african-americans-in-appalachia.
[8] Webb, "African Americans in Appalachia."
[9] Cara Robinson, "An Exploration of Poverty in Central Appalachia: Questions of Culture, Industry, and Technology," *KOME,* 3:2, (July 2015), 76, https://doi.org/10.17646/kome.2015.26.
[10] Robinson, "An Exploration of Poverty in Central Appalachia," 76.
[11] Robinson, "An Exploration of Poverty in Central Appalachia," 76.
[12] Robinson, "An Exploration of Poverty in Central Appalachia," 76.
[13] Robinson, "An Exploration of Poverty in Central Appalachia," 76.
[14] Robinson, "An Exploration of Poverty in Central Appalachia," 76.
[15] Robinson, "An Exploration of Poverty in Central Appalachia," 76.
[16] Appalachian Regional Commission, "Appalachia Envisioned: A New Era of Opportunity | ARC Strategic Plan Fiscal Years 2022-2026." Appalachian Regional Commission, 2022, 12.
[17] Appalachian Regional Commission, "Appalachia Envisioned," 12.

[18] Appalachian Regional Commission, "Appalachia Envisioned, 12."
[19] Appalachian Regional Commission, "Appalachia Envisioned," 14.
[20] Robinson, "An Exploration of Poverty in Central Appalachia," 76.
[21] Michael Meit, Megan Heffernan, Erin Tanenbaum, and Topher Hoffmann, *Appalachian Diseases of Despair* (Bethesda, MD: Walsh Center Rural Health Analysis, 2017).
[22] Gopal K. Singh, Michael D. Kogan, and Rebecca T. Slifkin, "Widening Disparities in Infant Mortality and Life Expectancy between Appalachia and the Rest of the United States, 1990–2013," *Health Affairs,* 36:8, (2017), 1423–32. https://doi.org/10.1377/hlthaff.2016.1571.
[23] Bronner, *Encyclopedia of American Folklife* 754-756.
[24] Bill Brinkley and Mamie G. Shull, "Interview with Mamie G. Shull, 3 April 1973," Appalachian State University Libraries Digital Collections, accessed 4 November 2021, https://omeka.library.appstate.edu/items/show/34230.
[25] L. Moody, E. Satterwhite, and W. K. Bickel, "Substance Use in Rural Central Appalachia: Current Status and Treatment Considerations," *Rural Mental Health*, 41:2, (2017), 123–135. https://doi.org/10.1037/rmh0000064
[26] Nick Gillespie, "What It's Like To Treat Opioid Addiction in Appalachia," *Reason,* 52:11, (2021),44–51.
[27] Jennifer Reynolds and Kristin Mattson, "Communicating about Opioids in Appalachia - Challenges, Opportunities, and Best Practices" (Appalachian Regional Comm., 2017), 1-32.
[28] Reynolds and Mattson, "Communicating about Opioids in Appalachia," 1-32.
[29] Reynolds and Mattson, "Communicating about Opioids in Appalachia," 1-32.
[30] Chad Montrie, *To Save the Land and People: A History of Opposition to Surface Coal Mining in Appalachia* (Chapel Hill: University of North Carolina Press, 2003), 14.
[31] Montrie, *To Save the Land and People,* 15.
[32] Montrie, *To Save the Land and People,* 17.
[33] Robinson, "An Exploration of Poverty in Central Appalachia."
[34] Justin Nobel, "Revolt in West Virginia's Coal Country," *Rolling Stone* (25 June 2018), https://www.rollingstone.com/politics/politics-news/revolt-in-west-virginias-coal-country-627943/.
[35] Jared Lee. Interview by Madison Lee. Personal Interview. Charleston, SC, 20 February 2022.

[36] Nobel, "Revolt in West Virginia's Coal Country."
[37] Sandra Slater, "Company Towns." History 210: History of Appalachia, lecture at College of Charleston, Charleston, SC, 2021.
[38] Slater, "Company Towns."
[39] Jessica Wilkerson, "'I'm Fighting for My Own Children That I'm Raising Up': Women, Labor, and Protest in Harlan County," in *To Live Here, You Have to Fight: How Women Led Appalachian Movements for Social Justice* (Urbana: University of Illinois Press, 2019), 149.
[40] Wilkerson, "I'm Fighting for My Own Children That I'm Raising Up," 153-167.
[41] Wilkerson, "I'm Fighting for My Own Children That I'm Raising Up," 167.
[42] "West Virginia Marriages, 1853–1970." Index. FamilySearch, Salt Lake City, Utah, 2008, 2009. Digital images of originals housed in County Courthouses in various counties throughout West Virginia. Marriage records.
[43] Year: 1930; Census Place: Marsh Fork, Raleigh, West Virginia; Page: 11B; Enumeration District: 0004; FHL microfilm: 2342286.
[44] Jared Lee. Interview by Madison Lee. Personal Interview. Charleston, 20 February 2022.
[45] Year: 1940; Census Place: Pike, Kentucky; Roll: m-t0627-01351; Page: 15B; Enumeration District: 98-27.
[46] Jared Lee. Interview by Madison Lee. Personal Interview. Charleston, 20 February 2022.
[47] U.S., World War II Navy, Marine Corps, and Coast Guard Casualties, 1941-1945 [database on-line]. Lehi, UT, USA: Ancestry.com Operations Inc, 2007.
[48] Jared Lee. Interview by Madison Lee. Personal Interview. Charleston, February 20, 2022.
[49] Carol A.B Giesen, "Living Day By Day," in *Coal Miners' Wives: Portraits of Endurance* (Lexington: University Press of Kentucky, 2015), 63-68.
[50] Giesen, "Living Day By Day," 5-8.
[51] Wilkerson, "I'm Fighting for My Own Children That I'm Raising Up," 169.
[52] "Receives a Degree," *The Raleigh Register* (Beckley, WV), 13 June 1955.
[53] Jared Lee. Interview by Madison Lee. Personal Interview. Charleston, 20 February 2022.

[54] Virginia, U.S., Marriage Records, 1936-2014 [database on-line]. Provo, UT, USA: Ancestry.com Operations, Inc., 2015.
[55] Jared Lee. Interview by Madison Lee. Personal Interview. Charleston, 20 February 2022.
[56] Jared Lee. Interview by Madison Lee. Personal Interview. Charleston, 20 February 2022.
[57] E. Arias, J.Q. Xu, B. Tejada-Vera, B. Bastian, U.S. state life tables, *National Vital Statistics Reports*, 70:18 (2019), DOI: https://dx.doi.org/10.15620/cdc:113251.
[58] Jared Lee. Interview by Madison Lee. Personal Interview. Charleston, February 20, 2022.
[59] "Dr. John D. Lee." The Raleigh Register (Beckley, WV), 11 November 1966.
[60] Claude A. Frazier, "Coalfield Doctors," *The West Virginia Encyclopedia*. 10 September 2010. Accessed 16 March 2022.
[61] Frazier, "Coalfield Doctors."
[62] Jared Lee. Interview by Madison Lee. Personal Interview. Charleston, 20 February 2022.
[63] Alan Derickson, "PART OF THE YELLOW DOG: U.S. COAL MINERS' OPPOSITION TO THE COMPANY DOCTOR SYSTEM, 1936-1946." *International Journal of Health Services* 19:4, (1989), 709.
[64] Frazier, "Coalfield Doctors."
[65] Derickson, "PART OF THE YELLOW DOG," 710-711.
[66] Derickson, "PART OF THE YELLOW DOG," 717.
[67] Jared Lee. Interview by Madison Lee. Personal Interview. Charleston, 20 February 2022.
[68] Jared Lee. Interview by Madison Lee. Personal Interview. Charleston, 20 February 2022.
[69] "Sylvester PTA Elects Officers," *The Beckley Post-Herald* (Beckley, WV), 14 September 1973.
[70] Jared Lee. Interview by Madison Lee. Personal Interview. Charleston, 20 February 2022.
[71] "Dr. John D. Lee Files For House" Beckley Post-Herald. 31 January 1956.
[72] Jared Lee. Interview by Madison Lee. Personal Interview. Charleston, 20 February 2022.
[73] Elizabeth Catte, *What You Are Getting Wrong about Appalachia* 27 (Cleveland: Belt Publishing, 2019), 27.
[74] Catte, *What You Are Getting Wrong about Appalachia*, 27.

[75] Catte, *What You Are Getting Wrong about Appalachia*, 27.
[76] Catte, *What You Are Getting Wrong about Appalachia*, 23.
[77] Catte, *What You Are Getting Wrong about Appalachia*, 23.
[78] Catte, *What You Are Getting Wrong about Appalachia*, 23.
[79] Catte, *What You Are Getting Wrong about Appalachia*, 27.
[80] "Racial Anxiety," *Perception Institute*, 26 February 2020, https://perception.org/research/racial-anxiety/.
[81] Catte, *What You Are Getting Wrong about Appalachia*, 28.
[82] Catte, *What You Are Getting Wrong about Appalachia*, 28.
[83] Larissa MacFarquhar. "In the Heart of Trump Country," *The New Yorker*, 3 October 2016.
[84] Leah W. Grohsgal, "Keeping Tradition Alive: Taking Steps to Preserve Appalachian Folk Culture," *The National Endowment for the Humanities*, 11 April 2016, https://www.neh.gov/divisions/preservation/featured-project/keeping-tradition-alive-taking-steps-preserve-appalachian-folk-culture.
[85] Grohsgal, "Keeping Tradition Alive."
[86] Grohsgal, "Keeping Tradition Alive."
[87] Catte, *What You Are Getting Wrong about Appalachia*, 22.
[88] Catte, *What You Are Getting Wrong about Appalachia*, 22.

**Endnotes for Chapter 2**

[1] "Marriage of Thomas Flynn and Sarah Kennedy," Georgia, Marriage Records, 1828-1978.
[2] U.S. Census Bureau. Population Report. 1860. Georgia Militia District 589, Georgia; Page: 655.
[3] U.S. Census Bureau. Population Report. 1850. District 89, Upson, Georgia; Roll: 85, Page: 298b.
[4] "Thomaston City." Thomaston City, Upson County, Georgia (GA). Accessed 22 April 2022. www.livingplaces.com/GA/Upson_County/Thomaston_City.html.
[5] Virginia Crilley, "Upson County: Militia Districts." Upson County, gagenweb project page -- land. Accessed 22 April 2022. https://sites.rootsweb.com/~gaupson/land.htm.
[6] "Upson County History: Hootenville." Upson County history - Georgia; Accessed 22 April 2022. http://www.usgennet.org/usa/ga/county/fulton/upsonhistory/.
[7] U.S., Civil War Soldier Records and Profiles, 1861-1865.

[8] "Battle Unit Details." National Parks Service. U.S. Department of the Interior. Accessed 22 April 2022. https://www.nps.gov/civilwar/search-battle-units-detail.htm?battleUnitCode=CGA0046RI.
[9] Roster of the Confederate Soldiers of Georgia, Vol 4, p. 930.
[10] U.S. Census Bureau. Population Report. 1870, Upson, Georgia; Roll: M593:179; Page: 77B.
[11] U.S. Census Bureau. Population Report. 1880, Kennesaw, Cobb, GA; Roll: 141; Page: 82A; Enumeration District 031.
[12] "Marriage of James Flynn and Rebecca Hudgens," Cobb County Marriage Records, Book D, Page 152, Entry 303.
[13] U.S. Census Bureau. Population Report. 1900, Oregon, Cobb, Georgia; Page 1; Enumeration District: 0044.
[14] Pamela F. Keller, interviewed by Chris Cone, 11 April 2022.
[15] U.S. Social Security Applications & Claims Index, 1936-2007.
[16] U.S. Census Bureau. Population Report. 1910. Cobb, GA; Roll: T624_180; Page: 14A; Enumeration District: 0043.
[17] Pamela F. Keller, interviewed by Chris Cone, 11 April 2022.
[18] U.S. Census Bureau. Agricultural Schedule, 1870, Subdivision 126, Union, Georgia; Archive Collection Number: T1137; Roll: T1137:8; Line: 7.
[19] U.S. WW1 Draft Registration Card, Lucious L Flynn, Georgia, Cobb, Roll: 1557016.
[20] Census Bureau. Population Report. 1930. Militia District 898, Cobb, GA; Page: 20A; Enumeration District: 0018.
[21] Pamela F. Keller, interview by Chris Cone, 11 April 2022.
[22] Social Security Index, Number: 253-30-7607; Issue State: Georgia; Issue Date: Before 1951.
[23] Pamela F. Keller, interview by Chris Cone, 11 April 2022.
[24] U.S. WWII Draft Registration Card, Luther Flynn, 1940-47.
[25] U.S. Marine Corps Muster Rolls, 1798-1958, Luther Flynn.
[26] Pamela F. Keller, interview by Chris Cone, 11 April 2022.
[27] South Carolina Department of Archives and History; Columbia, South Carolina, Certificates of Death; Year Range: 1966-1967; Death County or Certificate Range: 03007-04988.
[28] "James Owenby & Ola King," Georgia, Marriage Records, 1828-1978.
[29] U.S. Census Bureau, Population Report, 1920. Cobb, Georgia; Roll: T625_244; Page: 5B; Enumeration District: 43.

[30] U.S. Census Bureau. Population Report, 1910. Gumlog, Union, Georgia; Roll: T624_209; Page: 11 B; Enumeration District: 0150.
[31] U.S. Census Bureau. Population Report, 1920. Cobb, Georgia; Roll: m-t0627-00658; Page: 9A; Enumeration District: 33-22.
[32] Georgia Health Department, Office of Vital Records; Georgia, USA; Indexes of Vital Records for Georgia: Deaths, 1919-1998; Certificate Number: 005450.
[33] Bounty Land Warrant Applications Index, National Archives,1836.
[34] Plat for 742 Acres on Penny Creek, SC Department of Archives and History, Dec. 8, 1836. Series: S213190, Volume: 41, Page: 144.
[35] Bounty Land Warrant Applications Index, n.
[36] Rogers W. Young, "Fort Marion during the Seminole War 1835-1842." *The Florida Historical Society Quarterly* 13:4, (1935), 193–223.
[37] Patricia Bauer, ed. "Second Seminole War." *Encyclopedia Britannica.* Accessed 22 April 2022. https://www.britannica.com/event/Second-Seminole-War.
[38] "Osceola: Seminole Leader," *Encyclopedia Britannica.* Accessed 22 April 2022. https://www.britannica.com/biography/Osceola-Seminole-leader.
[39] U.S. Census Bureau. Population Report. 1850. Roll: 851; Page 262b.
[40] U.S. Census Bureau. Population Report. 1860. Roll: M653 1218; Page: 368.
[41] U.S. Census Bureau. Federal Slave Schedules, 1860. Series Number: M653, Group 29.
[42] Compiled Service Records of Confederate Soldiers Who Served in Organizations from the State of South Carolina 1864
[43] Records of the Field Offices for the State of South Carolina, Bureau of Refugees, Freedmen, and Abandoned Lands, 1865-1872; NARA Series Number: M1910; NARA Reel Number: 103.
[44] Joseph D. Reid, "Sharecropping in History and Theory." Agricultural History 49:2, (1975), 426–40.
[45] U.S. Census Bureau. Agricultural Report. 1880. Verdier, Colleton, South Carolina; Archive Collection Number: AD270; Roll: 9; Page 7; Line: 3.
[46] U.S. Census Bureau. Population Report. 1880. Burns, Colleton, South Carolina; Roll: 1226; Page 344B; Enumeration District: 102.
[47] U.S. Census Bureau. Population Report. 1900. Burns, Dorchester, SC; Page 9; Enumeration District: 0065.

[48] U.S. Census Bureau. Population Report. 1900. Burns, Dorchester, South Carolina; Roll: 1526; Page: 9; Enumeration District: 0065.
[49] U.S. Census Bureau. Population Report. 1910. Georgetown, South Carolina; Roll: T624_1458; Page: 27A; Enumeration District: 0037.
[50] U.S. WWI Draft Registration Card, John H. Cone, 1917-18.
[51] Milton M. Cone, interview by Chris Cone, 3 April 2022
[52] U.S. Census Bureau. Population Report. 1930. Dorchester, South Carolina; Page: 8B; Enumeration District 0008.
[53] Milton M. Cone, interview by Chris Cone, 3 April 2022.

**Endnotes for Chapter 3**
[1] Jean Clark Boyd, *A Pictorial Timeline of Graniteville, South Carolina 1845-1996.* (South Carolina: Horse Creek Historical Society, 2004), 1; Tom Downey, "Riparian Rights and Manufacturing in Antebellum South Carolina: William Gregg and the Origins of the 'Industrial Mind'," *The Journal of Southern History,* 65:1, (1999): 78. doi:10.2307/2587732.
[2] Tom Downey, "Riparian Rights and Manufacturing in Antebellum South Carolina: William Gregg and the Origins of the 'Industrial Mind'," *The Journal of Southern History,* 65:1, (1999), 79-80. doi:10.2307/2587732.
[3] Broadus Mitchell, *William Gregg: Factory Master of the Old South* (Chapel Hill: University of North Carolina Press, 1928), 23-25.
[4] Mary Anne Duncan, Daniel Drociuk, Amy Belflower-Thomas, David Van Sickle, James J. Gibson, Claire Youngblood, & W. Randolph Daley, "Follow-Up Assessment of Health Consequences after a Chlorine Release from a Train Derailment- Graniteville, SC, 2005," *Journal of Medical Toxicology*, 7, 85-91, 2 February 2011.
[5] See Nathaniel R. Walker, *Victorian Visions of Suburban Utopia: Abandoning Babylon* (Oxford: Oxford University Press, 2020).
[6] Ophélie Siméon, *Robert Owen's Experiment at New Lanark: From Paternalism to Socialism* (Spring International Publishing), 88-89.
[7] Siméon, *Robert Owen's Experiment at New Lanark*, 53.
[8] Donald F. Carmony and Josephine M. Elliot, "New Harmony, Indiana: Robert Owen's Seedbed for Utopia," *Indiana Magazine of History,* 76:3, (Indiana University Press, 1980), 164-165,
[9] Timothy R. Mahoney, "The Small City in American History," Trustees of Indiana University, 2003. https://history.unl.edu/docs/Faculty/pdfs/IMH2.pdf.

[10] See Miles Orvell, *The Death and Life of Main Street: Small towns in American Memory, Space, and Community* (Chapel Hill: University of North Carolina Press, 2012).
[11] Robbie Davis, "Public History in Small-Town America: Twenty Years of Museum on Main Street," *The Public Historian* 36:4, (2014), 51–70. https://doi.org/10.1525/tph.2014.36.4.51.
[12] Davis, "Public History in Small-Town America," 51–70.
[13] Karen Good, "Preservation of Small-town Character in The Town Center of Rutland, Massachusetts," University of Massachusetts Amherst, May 2002. https://scholarworks.umass.edu/cgi/viewcontent.cgi?article=1035&context=larp_ms_projects.
[14] Preston Willett, "Group looks to bring Graniteville into 21st century," *WRDW, Gray Television*, 12 January 2017, https://www.wrdw.com/content/news/Group-looks-to-bring-Graniteville-into-21st-century-410577355.html.
[15] Joe Sugarman, "The Town of Graniteville, South Carolina, Sees its Future in its Historic Buildings," Preservation Magazine, National Trust for Historic Preservation, Spring 2019, https://savingplaces.org/stories/the-town-of-graniteville-south-carolina-sees-its-future-in-its-historic-buildings#.YkxtgyjMLIX.
[16] Zell Seymour in discussion with the author, January 2022.
[17] 1900 U.S. Federal Census.
[18] Zell Seymour in discussion with the author, January 2022.
[19] A.K. Roy Chouldhury, *Textile Preparation and Dying* (New Hampshire: Science Publishers, 2006), 131.
[20] Jim Seymour in discussion with the author, January 2022.
[21] Zell Seymour in discussion with the author, January 2022.
[22] Zell Seymour in discussion with the author, January 2022.
[23] Willett, "Group looks to bring Graniteville into 21st century"
[24] Joe Sugarman, "The Town of Graniteville, South Carolina, Sees its Future in its Historic Buildings," *Preservation Magazine*, (Spring 2019), https://savingplaces.org/stories/the-town-of-graniteville-south-carolina-sees-its-future-in-its-historic-buildings#.YkxtgyjMLIX.
[25] Jim Seymour in discussion with the author, January 2022.
[26] Jim Seymour in discussion with the author, January 2022.
[27] Jim Seymour in discussion with the author, January 2022.
[28] Jim Seymour in discussion with the author, January 2022.

[29] Becky Henshaw "Graniteville: Storybook town was built for workers at factory in 1846 Horse Creek Valley," May 9 1982. In the Aiken County Historical Museum vertical file, Aiken, SC, accessed February 2022.
[30] Edward H., "Historical sites of Graniteville Area," (1976): 9-10, in the Aiken County Historical Museum vertical file, Aiken, SC.
[31] "Miss Jo's Candy Store," in the Aiken County Historical Museum vertical file, Aiken, South Carolina, accessed February 2022.
[32] Edward H., "Historical sites of Graniteville Area."
[33] Edward H., "Historical sites of Graniteville Area."
[34] Edward H., "Historical sites of Graniteville Area."
[35] Jim Seymour in discussion with the author, January 2022.
[36] Becky Henshaw "Graniteville: Storybook town was built for workers at factory in 1846 Horse Creek Valley," 9 May 1982. In the Aiken County Historical Museum vertical file, Aiken, SC, accessed February 2022.
[37] *Graniteville Bulletin*, published by Graniteville Company and its Employees. Aiken County Historical Museum vertical file, Aiken, South Carolina, accessed February 2022.
[38] *Graniteville Bulletin*, published by Graniteville Company and its Employees. Aiken County Historical Museum vertical file, Aiken, SC, accessed February 2022.
[39] Mae Steadman, "A History of Graniteville." Aiken County Historical Museum vertical file, Aiken, SC, accessed February 2022.
[40] Boyd, *A Pictorial Timeline of Graniteville,* 32. Also see Steadman, "A History of Graniteville.".
[41] Steadman, "A History of Graniteville," 8.
[42] Walker, *Victorian Visions of Suburban Utopia*, 69-71.
[43] Walker, *Victorian Visions of Suburban Utopia*, 68.
[44] Robert Owen, *A Development of the Principles and Plans on which to Establish Self-supporting Home Colonies* (London: Home Colonization Society, 1841).
[45] Donald F. Carmony and Josephine M. Elliot, "New Harmony, Indiana: Robert Owen's Seedbed for Utopia," *Indiana Magazine of History,* 76:3, (1980), 162-165,
[46] Walker, *Victorian Visions of Suburban Utopia*, 11.
[47] Carmony and Elliot, "New Harmony, Indiana: Robert Owen's Seedbed for Utopia," 164-165,
[48] Boyd, *A Pictorial Timeline of Graniteville,* 1.

[49] Owen, *A Development of the Principles and Plans on which to Establish Self-supporting Home Colonies,* 2.
[50] Owen, *A Development of the Principles and Plans on which to Establish Self-supporting Home Colonies,* 6,
[51] Dorothy K. MacDowell, "Historical sites of Graniteville Area," 5, Aiken County Historical Museum vertical file, Aiken, SC.
[52] "Rice Reverses 'Token' Decision," *NewspaperArticle*, (Aiken Journal and Review*)*, 28 February 1935.
[53] "Object Record," Aiken County Historical Museum, Catalog Number 2005.13.01a, accessed 13 April 2022, https://achm.catalogaccess.com/objects/2788.
[54] Zell Seymour in discussion with the author, March 2022.
[55] "Rice Reverses 'Token' Decision," *Aiken Journal and Review,* 28 February 1935.
[56] Owen, *A Development of the Principles and Plans on which to Establish Self-supporting Home Colonies,* 3.
[57] Owen, *A Development of the Principles and Plans on which to Establish Self-supporting Home Colonies,* 3.
[58] Owen, *A Development of the Principles and Plans on which to Establish Self-supporting Home Colonies,* 7.
[59] Zell Seymour in discussion with the author, January 2022.
[60] Becky Henshaw, "Graniteville: Storybook town was built for workers at factory in 1846 Horse Creek Valley," 9 May 1982. Aiken County Historical Museum vertical file, Aiken, SC.
[61] Martin Wiener, *English Culture & the Decline of the Industrial Spirit,1850-1980* (Cambridge: Cambridge University Press, 2004), 64,
[62] Ophélie Siméon, *Robert Owen's Experiment at New Lanark: From Paternalism to Socialism* (Spring International Publishing AG), 4.
[63] Siméon, *Robert Owen's Experiment at New Lanark.*
[64] Siméon, *Robert Owen's Experiment at New Lanark.*
[65] Siméon, *Robert Owen's Experiment at New Lanark.*
[66] Siméon, *Robert Owen's Experiment at New Lanark.*
[67] See Walker, *Victorian Visions of Suburban Utopia.*
[68] A.W. Pugin, *Contrasts,* (New York: Cambridge University Press, 1841/2013), 51.
[69] Pugin, *Contrasts,* 7, 33.
[70] Wiener, *English Culture & the Decline of the Industrial Spirit,* 64.
[71] Wiener, *English Culture & the Decline of the Industrial Spirit,* 29.
[72] Wiener, *English Culture & the Decline of the Industrial Spirit,* 29.

[73] Boyd, *A Pictorial Timeline of Graniteville*, 1.
[74] Boyd, *A Pictorial Timeline of Graniteville,* 11.
[75] Zell Seymour in discussion with the author, March 2022.
[76] Tom Downey, "Riparian Rights and Manufacturing in Antebellum South Carolina: William Gregg and the Origins of the 'Industrial Mind'," *The Journal of Southern History,* 65:1, (1999), 79-80. doi:10.2307/2587732.
[77] Edward H., "Historical sites of Graniteville Area," (1976), 9-10, Aiken County Historical Museum vertical file.
[78] "National Register Properties in South Carolina: Graniteville Historic District, Aiken County (Graniteville)," South Carolina Department of Archives and History, accessed 31 March 2022, www.nationalregister.sc.gov/aiken/S10817702011/index.htm.
[79] Boyd, *A Pictorial Timeline of Graniteville.*
[80] Sue McLaughlin and Sharon McLaughlin, *Reflections of Graniteville* (Graniteville, SC: 1976).
[81] Boyd, *A Pictorial Timeline of Graniteville.*
[82] Brian Sanders in discussion with the author, January 2022.
[83] Jim Seymour in discussion with the author, January 2022.

**Endnotes for Chapter 4**

[1] See the citations below for the sources covered in the Prior Academic Research section.
[2] "The Palatine Germans (U.S. National Park Service)." National Parks Service. U.S. Department of the Interior. Accessed 1 February 2022. https://www.nps.gov/articles/000/the-palatine-germans.htm.
[3] History.com Editors. "Thirty Years' War." History.com. A&E Television Networks, November 9, 2009. https://www.history.com/topics/reformation/thirty-years-war.
[4] Nelson Greene, "Mohawk Valley and Schenectady 1701-1713," in *History of the Mohawk Valley: Gateway to the West, 1614-1925, Covering the Six Counties of Schenectady, Schoharie, Montgomery, Fulton, Herkimer and Oneida* (Chicago, IL: S.J. Clarke Pub. Co., 1925), 436.
[5] "Klock Family History." Klock Name Meaning & Klock Family History at Ancestry.com®. Accessed 17 February 2022. https://www.ancestry.com/name-origin?surname=Klock.
[6] Knittle, *The Early Eighteenth Century Palatine Emigration,* 143.
[7] Knittle, *The Early Eighteenth Century Palatine Emigration,* 146.
[8] Knittle, *The Early Eighteenth Century Palatine Emigration*, 141.

[9] Knittle,*The Early Eighteenth Century Palatine Emigration,*141-42.
[10] Knittle,*The Early Eighteenth Century Palatine Emigration,*141-42.
[11] Knittle,*The Early Eighteenth Century Palatine Emigration,*146-47.
[12] Hank Jones, *The Palatine Families of New York: A Study of the German Immigrants Who Arrived in Colonial New York in 1710* (Universal City, CA: H.Z. Jones, 1985).
[13] Jones, *The Palatine Families of New York*, xiii.
[14] Lou D. MacWethy, "Governor Hunter's Ration Lists," in *The Book of Names, Especially Relating to the Early Palatines and the First Settlers in the Mohawk Valley*, 68. Baltimore, MD: Reprinted for Clearfield by Genealogical Pub. Co., 2007.
[15] Jones, *The Palatine Families of New York*, 289.
[16] Knittle, *The Early Eighteenth Century Palatine Emigration*, 152.
[17] Jones, *The Palatine Families of New York,* xiii.
[18] Knittle, *The Early Eighteenth Century Palatine Emigration*, 296.
[19] Knittle, *The Early Eighteenth Century Palatine Emigration*, 296.
[20] Lou D.MacWethy, "The Kocherthal Records," in *The Book of Names, Especially Relating to the Early Palatines and the First Settlers in the Mohawk Valley* (Baltimore, MD: Reprinted for Clearfield by Genealogical Pub. Co., 2007).
[21] Jones, *The Palatine Families of New York,* xiii.
[22] Jones, *The Palatine Families of New York,* xiv.
[23] "Legislative Acts/Legal Proceedings." *Boston News-Letter* (Boston, Massachusetts), no. 386, September 10, 1711: [1]. *Readex: America's Historical Newspapers*.
[24] Jones, *The Palatine Families of New York,* xiv.
[25] Knittle, *The Early Eighteenth Century Palatine Emigration*, 215.
[26] MacWethy, *The Book of Names,* 3.
[27] Knittle, *The Early Eighteenth Century Palatine Emigration*, 189.
[28] Berry, "Life on the Home Front," 79.
[29] Knittle, *The Early Eighteenth Century Palatine Emigration*, 197.
[30] David L. Preston, "George Klock, the Canajoharie Mohawks, and the Good Ship Sir William Johnson: Land, Legitimacy, and Community in the Eighteenth-Century Mohawk Valley." *New York History,* 86: 4, (2005), 479.
[31] Knittle, *The Early Eighteenth Century Palatine Emigration*, 202.
[32] Knittle, *The Early Eighteenth Century Palatine Emigration,* 204.
[33] Preston, David L. *Texture of Contact: European and Indian Settler Communities on the Frontiers of Iroquoia, 1667-1783* (Lincoln: University of Nebraska Press, 2009), 85.

[34] Preston, "George Klock, the Canajoharie Mohawks, and the Good Ship Sir William Johnson," 476.
[35] "Maria Margaretha Schopfer Klock (1672-1721)" Find a Grave. Accessed 22 February 2022. https://www.findagrave.com/memorial/184783709/maria-margaretha-klock.
[36] Nelson Greene, "Mohawk Valley History From 1713-1744" in *History of the Mohawk Valley* (Chicago: S.J.Clarke Pub., 1925), 517.
[37] Preston, "George Klock, the Canajoharie Mohawks, and the Good Ship Sir William Johnson," 480.
[38] Preston, *Texture of Contact*, 85.
[39] "Hendrick J. 'Henry' Klock (1693-1759) - Find a..." Find a Grave. Accessed 24 February 2022. https://www.findagrave.com/memorial/185033779/hendrick-j.-klock.
[40] "Jacomyntie Mohawk Indian (1700-1759) - Find a..." Find a Grave. Accessed 1 March 2022. https://www.findagrave.com/memorial/185034145/jacomyntie-mohawk_indian.
[41] Eric Hinderaker, *The Two Hendricks: Unraveling a Mohawk Mystery* (Cambridge, MA: Harvard University Press, 2011), 40.
[42] "Excerpts about the Town of Palatine Part 2." Early History Town of Palatine Montgomery County NY Genealogy. Accessed 1 March 2022. http://montgomery.nygenweb.net/palatine/palexcerpts2.html.
[43] "Klock's Purchase." Map. *The Maps of the Commissioners of Forfeitures* #AO273. Portfolio E. Map #865.
[44] *The Mohawk Valley and the American Revolution* (Albany: State of New York, Parks & Recreation, 1972), 3.
[45] *The Mohawk Valley and the American Revolution* (Albany: State of New York, Parks & Recreation, 1972), 3.
[46] John J. Vrooman, *Forts and Firesides of the Mohawk Country, New York* (Johnstown, NY: Baronet Litho Co., 1951), 233.
[47] "Klock's Purchase." Map. *The Maps of the Commissioners of Forfeitures* #AO273. Portfolio E. Map #865.
[48] Green, *History of the Mohawk Valley*, 558.
[49] Fort Klock Historic Restoration. "Welcome to Fort Klock Historic Restoration." Fort Klock Historic Restoration. Accessed 3 March 2022. https://fortklockrestoration.org/.
[50] Charles W. Snell, "National Register of Historic Places Nomination Form: Fort Klock", Washington D.C: National Park Service, 1972, 3.

[51] AJ Berry, "Three Fort Klocks" in *A Time of Terror*, 294-295.
[52] "Sir William Johnson (U.S. National Park Service)." National Parks Service. U.S. Department of the Interior. Accessed 22 March 2022. https://www.nps.gov/people/sir-william-johnson.htm.
[53] Gabriella M. Rowsam and David L Preston. The Klocks and the Mohawk Valley. Personal, 23 March 2022.
[54] Preston, "George Klock, the Canajoharie Mohawks, and the Good Ship Sir William Johnson," 481.
[55] Preston, "George Klock, the Canajoharie Mohawks, and the Good Ship Sir William Johnson," 481.
[56] Preston, *Texture of Contact*, 178.
[57] Preston, *Texture of Contact*, 178.
[58] Preston, *Texture of Contact*, 188.
[59] Preston, *Texture of Contact*, 184.
[60] MacWethy, *The Book of Names,* 149.
[61] Berry, "Introduction" in *A Time of Terror*, 9.
[62] Preston, "George Klock, the Canajoharie Mohawks, and the Good Ship Sir William Johnson," 488.
[63] Gabriella M. Rowsam and David L Preston. The Klocks and the Mohawk Valley. Personal, 23 March 2022.
[64] Preston, "George Klock, the Canajoharie Mohawks, and the Good Ship Sir William Johnson," 486.
[65] Preston, "George Klock, the Canajoharie Mohawks, and the Good Ship Sir William Johnson," 485.
[66] Preston, "George Klock, the Canajoharie Mohawks, and the Good Ship Sir William Johnson," 487.
[67] Preston, "George Klock, the Canajoharie Mohawks, and the Good Ship Sir William Johnson," 486-487.
[68] Gabriella M. Rowsam and David L Preston. The Klocks and the Mohawk Valley. Personal, 23 March 2022.
[69] Preston, "George Klock, the Canajoharie Mohawks, and the Good Ship Sir William Johnson, 488.
[70] Preston, "George Klock, the Canajoharie Mohawks, and the Good Ship Sir William Johnson," 489.
[71] Preston, "George Klock, the Canajoharie Mohawks, and the Good Ship Sir William Johnson," 489.
[72] Preston, "George Klock, the Canajoharie Mohawks, and the Good Ship Sir William Johnson," 489.
[73] Preston, "George Klock, the Canajoharie Mohawks, and the Good Ship Sir William Johnson," 493.

[74] Gabriella M. Rowsam and David L Preston. The Klocks and the Mohawk Valley. Personal, 23 March 2022.
[75] Preston, "George Klock, the Canajoharie Mohawks, and the Good Ship Sir William Johnson," 492.
[76] Preston, "George Klock, the Canajoharie Mohawks, and the Good Ship Sir William Johnson," 492.
[77] Preston, "George Klock, the Canajoharie Mohawks, and the Good Ship Sir William Johnson," 492.
[78] Preston, "George Klock, the Canajoharie Mohawks, and the Good Ship Sir William Johnson," 493.
[79] History.com Editors. "Proclamation of 1763." History.com. A&E Television Networks, 27 October 2009. https://www.history.com/topics/native-american-history/1763-proclamation-of.
[80] Preston, *Texture of Contact*, 180.
[81] Preston, "George Klock, the Canajoharie Mohawks, and the Good Ship Sir William Johnson," 494.
[82] Preston, "George Klock, the Canajoharie Mohawks, and the Good Ship Sir William Johnson," 495.
[83] Preston, "George Klock, the Canajoharie Mohawks, and the Good Ship Sir William Johnson," 474, 495.
[84] Milo Nellis, "The Mohawk Valley Declaration of Independence" in *Old Palatine Church* (St. Johnsville, NY: Press of the Enterprise and News, 1930), 36.
[85] Nellis, "The Mohawk Valley Declaration of Independence," 36.
[86] Nellis, "The Mohawk Valley Declaration of Independence," 36.
[87] History.com Editors. "Committees of Correspondence." *History.com. A&E Television Networks*, 27 October 2009. https://www.history.com/topics/american-revolution/committees-of-correspondence.
[88] Colonel Jacob Klock's will is located in the New York, U.S., Wills and Probate Records, 1659-1999, New York County, District and Probate Courts, Ancestry.com.
[89] John Johnson, *Orderly Book of Sir John Johnson During the Oriskany Campaign, 1776-1777* (New York: J. Munsell, 1882), 163.
[90] Snell, "National Register of Historic Places Nomination Form: Fort Klock", 21.
[91] Snell, "National Register of Historic Places Nomination Form: Fort Klock", 21.

[92] Preston, "George Klock, the Canajoharie Mohawks, and the Good Ship Sir William Johnson," 499.
[93] Snell, "National Register of Historic Places Nomination Form: Fort Klock", 3.
[94] Johannes Klock information found in the U.S., Sons of the American Revolution Membership Applications, 1889-1970, Ancestry.com, National Society of the Sons of the American Revolution. Microfilm, 508 rolls.
[95] Nelson Greene, "1778 Mohawk Valley Raids," in *History of the Mohawk Valley: Gateway to the West, 1614-1925* (Chicago: S.J. Clarke Pub. Co., 1925), 887.
[96] Greene, "1778 Mohawk Valley Raids", 890.
[97] Snell, "National Register of Historic Places Nomination Form: Fort Klock", 3-5.
[98] Greene, "1776-1777, Mohawk Valley Revolutionary Forts," 781.
[99] "Fort Klock." Visit Sacandaga. Accessed 30 March 2022. http://www.visitsacandaga.com/portfolio/fort-klock/.
[100] Snell, "National Register of Historic Places Nomination Form: Fort Klock," 5.
[101] Snell, "National Register of Historic Places Nomination Form: Fort Klock," 5.
[102] *The Mohawk Valley and the American Revolution* (Albany: State of New York, Parks & Recreation, 1972), 28.
[103] Snell, "National Register of Historic Places Nomination Form: Fort Klock," 21.
[104] "Legislative Acts/Legal Proceedings." *Gazette of the United States* (New York), 2:43, (8 September 1790), 588.
[105] Preston, "George Klock, the Canajoharie Mohawks, and the Good Ship Sir William Johnson," 498.
[106] Snell, "National Register of Historic Places Nomination Form: Fort Klock," 3.
[107] National Archives and Records Administration. Accessed 13 March 2022. https://catalog.archives.gov/search?q=fortified+homestead&f.ancestorNaIds=71998949.
[108] Snell, "National Register of Historic Places Nomination Form: Fort Johnson."
[109] Fort Klock Historic Restoration. "Welcome to Fort Klock Historic Restoration." *Fort Klock Historic Restoration.* Accessed 3 March 2022. https://fortklockrestoration.org/.

[110] Snell, “National Register of Historic Places Nomination Form: Fort Klock,” 3.
[111] Berry, *A Time of Terror*, 297.
[112] Preston, “George Klock, the Canajoharie Mohawks, and the Good Ship Sir William Johnson,” 499.

**Endnotes to Chapter 5**
[1] Peter Lukianov, "Orthodox in Dixie: A Documentary About Russian Orthodox South Carolina," Executive Producer: Gregory Levitsky. *Eastern American Diocese ROCOR*. 2 January 2013. Video, 40:00. https://www.youtube.com/watch?v=lb6ZLx0qPNY.
[2] Fevronia K. Soumakis and Theodore G. Zervas, *Educating Greek Americans Historical Perspectives and Contemporary Pathways* (Cham: Springer International Publishing, 2020.), xiii
[3] “Rebetiko,” Representative List of the Intangible Cultural Heritage of Humanity. UNESCO, 2017.
“Mediterranean Diet.” Representative List of the Intangible Cultural Heritage of Humanity. UNESCO, 2013.
[4] George Sigalas, “Personal Memoirs.” (Unpublished Manuscript, Private Collection of Author, 2005.), 19
[5] Noah Sigalas, Interview: Michael Sigalas. 19 January 2022.
[6] Noah Sigalas, Interview: Michael Sigalas. 19 January 2022.
[7] Noah Sigalas, Interview: George Constantine Sigalas II. 19 January 2022.
[8] Eleni Andreouli, et al. “‘Europe’ in Greece: Lay Constructions of Europe in the Context of Greek Immigration Debates.” *Journal of Community & Applied Social Psychology*, 27:2, (2017), 158–68. https://doi.org/10.1002/casp.2301.
[9] George Morris, *Charleston’s Greek Heritage* (Charleston, SC: The History Press, 2008).
[10] See Soumakis and. Zervas, *Educating Greek Americans Historical Perspectives and Contemporary Pathways*.
[11] Noah Sigalas, Interview: George Constantine Sigalas I. 2002.
[12] Noah Sigalas, Interview: George Constantine Sigalas III. 2018.
[13] Noah Sigalas, Interview: George Constantine Sigalas II. 19 January 2022.
[14] Noah Sigalas, Interview: Michael Sigalas. 19 January 2022; Walter Christmas, *King George of Greece*. (New York: McBride, Nast & Company, 1914), 401-407.

[15] George Sigalas, "Personal Memoirs." (Unpublished Manuscript, Private Collection of Author, 2005.), 7.
[16] Sigalas, "Personal Memoirs," 17.
[17] Sigalas, "Personal Memoirs," 17.
[18] Greg Young and Tom Meyers, "Hell's Kitchen: New York's Wild West." *The Bowery Boys: New York City History,* 17 August 2020.
[19] Sigalas, "Personal Memoirs," 15.
[20] Young and Meyers. "Hell's Kitchen: New York's Wild West."
[21] Mabel L. Walker, *Urban Blight and Slums* (New York: Russell & Russell Div. of Atheneum Publishers, 1971), 22-23
[22] Young and Meyers. "Hell's Kitchen: New York's Wild West."
[23] C.B. Whitehall, *What Progress Costs Milwaukee.* (Milwaukee: Author Published, 1935) 63, Qtd. in Mabel L. Walker, *Urban Blight and Slums* (New York: Russell & Russell Div. of Atheneum Publishers, 1971), 25.
[24] Young and Meyers. "Hell's Kitchen: New York's Wild West."
[25] Young and Meyers. "Hell's Kitchen: New York's Wild West;" George Sigalas, "Personal Memoirs." (Unpublished Manuscript, Private Collection of Author, 2005.)
[26] George Sigalas, "Personal Memoirs." (Unpublished Manuscript, Private Collection of Author, 2005.), 40-41
[27] "2 Jailed in Fight Fix," *Daily News* (New York), 13 February 1937.
[28] Walker, *Urban Blight and Slums*, 22-23.
[29] "About Us." *The Tenement Museum.* Lower East Side Tenement Museum. https://www.tenement.org/about-us/; Young and Meyers. "Hell's Kitchen: New York's Wild West.".
[30] Lisa Boehm and Steven H. Corey. *America's Urban History* (New York: Routledge, 2015), 273-279;
Mary E. Hayward, and Frank R. Shivers, *The Architecture of Baltimore*: An Illustrated History (Baltimore: Johns Hopkins University Press, 2004.), 286-294.
[31] Google Maps. "265 West Fortieth Avenue." Accessed 17 March 2022; George Sigalas, "Personal Memoirs." (Unpublished Manuscript, Private Collection of Author, 2005.), 15; 1915, New York State Census; 1920, United States Federal Census; 1925, New York State Census; 1930, United States Federal Census.
[32] Boehm and Corey, *America's Urban History*, 273-279.

[33] Irma Milstein and Paul Milstein, "Manhattan: 40th Street (West) - 8th Avenue" New York Public Library Digital Collections. Accessed 31 March 2022. https://digitalcollections.nypl.org/items/510d47dd-03b9-a3d9-e040-e00a18064a99.
[34] "Rebetiko," Representative List of the Intangible Cultural Heritage of Humanity. UNESCO, 2017.
"Mediterranean Diet." Representative List of the Intangible Cultural Heritage of Humanity. UNESCO, 2013.
[35] Henry P. Fairchild, *Greek Immigration to the United States* (New Haven, CT: Yale University Press, 1911), 46;
Soumakis and Zervas, *Educating Greek Americans Historical Perspectives and Contemporary Pathways*, x-xi.
[36] "Byzantine Chant." Representative List of the Intangible Cultural Heritage of Humanity. UNESCO, 2019.
[37] Kyle E. Haden, "Anti-Catholicism in U.S. History: A Proposal for a New Methodology." *American Catholic Studies,* 124:4, (2013), 31.
[38] Fairchild, *Greek Immigration to the United States*, 46.
[39] Soumakis and Zervas, *Educating Greek Americans Historical Perspectives and Contemporary Pathways,* x-xi.
[40] Noah Sigalas, Interview: Father Aristotle Papoulis. 5 May 2022; and Noah Sigalas, Interview: Father John Cox. 5 May 2022.

www.ingramcontent.com/pod-product-compliance
Lightning Source LLC
LaVergne TN
LVHW050636100826
845148LV00011B/1881